P9-EME-579

THE
FDR
STORY

By the Author

THE HELEN KELLER STORY
THE FDR STORY
THE WOODROW WILSON STORY

THE
FDR
STORY

Catherine Owens Peare

Thomas Y. Crowell Company
New York

Manufactured in the United States of America by the Vail-Ballou Press, Inc., Binghamton, New York

Library of Congress Catalog Card No. 62-11003

Third Printing

I am indebted to the late President's only daughter, Mrs. James A. Halsted; and to Miss Elizabeth B. Drewry, Director, Miss Margaret L. Suckley, Mr. Joseph W. Marshall, and Mr. Raymond H. Corry, at the Franklin D. Roosevelt Library in Hyde Park; all of whom read my entire manuscript for accuracy. I am also indebted for special advice and assistance to Miss May Lipton, Mr. Edward Gilmore, and Mr. Josef Berger of The National Foundation; Mr. Charles A. Phelan, Jr., Secretary-Treasurer at The Little White House; Mr. Robert F. Chaplin, Director of Public Information at the Georgia Warm Springs Foundation; Miss Lavinia Dobler, Librarian of Scholastic Magazines, Inc.; and to the librarians at the New York Academy of Medicine and at the Ingersoll Building of the Brooklyn Public Library.

I am grateful to the following for permission to use material from the works indicated below:

The Bobbs-Merrill Company, Inc.: *Franklin D. Roosevelt, A Career in Progressive Democracy*, copyright © 1931, 1959 by Ernest K. Lindley, reprinted by special permission of the publishers.

Brandt & Brandt: *Admiral Halsey's Story* by William F. Halsey and J. Bryan, III, 1947 (McGraw-Hill Book Company, Inc.).

Coward-McCann, Inc.: *Peabody of Groton*, copyright 1944 by Frank Ashburn.

Duell, Sloan & Pearce, Inc.: *F.D.R.: His Personal Letters*, vol. I copyright 1947 by Elliott Roosevelt, vol. II copyright 1948 by Elliott Roosevelt, vol. III copyright 1950 by Elliott Roosevelt; *As He Saw It*, copyright 1946 by Elliott Roosevelt.

Harcourt, Brace & World, Inc.: *Affectionately, F.D.R.*, © 1959 by James Roosevelt and Sidney Shalett; *Roosevelt, The Lion and the Fox* by James MacGregor Burns, 1956.

Harper & Brothers: *This Is My Story* by Eleanor Roosevelt, 1937; *This I Remember* by Eleanor Roosevelt, 1949; *The Politics of Woodrow Wilson*, edited by August Heckscher, 1956; *Working with Roosevelt* by Samuel I. Rosenman, 1952.

Houghton Mifflin Company: *The Crisis of the Old Order 1919–1933* by Arthur M. Schlesinger, Jr., 1957; *The Coming of the New Deal* by Arthur M. Schlesinger, Jr., 1959.

Little, Brown & Company: *Franklin D. Roosevelt*: vol. I, *The Apprenticeship*, vol. II, *The Ordeal*, by Frank Freidel, 1952 and 1954.

G. P. Putnam's Sons: *Mrs. R: The Life of Eleanor Roosevelt*, copyright © 1958 by Alfred Steinberg.

Mr. James Roosevelt for permission to reproduce the text of the telegram of his father's death.

Charles Scribner's Sons: *F.D.R., My Boss* by Grace Tully, 1949.

Simon and Schuster, Inc.: *Journey Through My Years*, copyright 1946 by James M. Cox.

The University of North Carolina Press: *The Wilson Era* by Josephus Daniels, 1944.

The World Publishing Company: *The Man Behind Roosevelt* by Lela Stiles, 1954; *Nothing to Fear, The Selected Addresses (1932–1945) of Franklin Delano Roosevelt*, edited by Ben D. Zevin, 1946.

Contents

1   BEGINNING AT HYDE PARK   1
2   SCHOOL BOY   15
3   COLLEGE MAN   38
4   STATE SENATOR   55
5   FROM ALBANY TO WASHINGTON   66
6   ASSISTANT SECRETARY OF THE NAVY   80
7   POLIO STRIKES   98
8   TOUCHING BOTTOM AND RISING   121
9   WARM SPRINGS INTERLUDE   136
10 GOVERNOR OF NEW YORK   150
11 ATTACKING THE DEPRESSION   171
12 OPPOSITION   188
13 GLOBAL WAR   205
14 TWO GREAT DREAMS COMING TRUE   226

    SELECTED BIBLIOGRAPHY   235
    INDEX   239

List of Illustrations

FOLLOWING PAGE 118

FDR at sixteen months
Franklin in his last year at Groton
FDR as a senior at Harvard
Mr. and Mrs. Franklin D. Roosevelt
  with their children, 1916
Churchill, Roosevelt, and Stalin at Yalta
Aerial view of Warm Springs, Georgia

Chapter One

Beginning at Hyde Park

THE HUDSON RIVER was gray with ice, and the trees along its bank were leafless on the winter morning that Franklin Delano Roosevelt was born. In the big house whose western windows looked down the long sweep of hill to the river his family moved about sober-faced with no thought for the season. Husband, doctor, nurse, servants, spoke in whispers.

"I didn't expect the little boy to be born alive, sir," the nurse admitted to Mr. James Roosevelt.

In the mahogany bed with its tall massive headboard, Sara Delano Roosevelt lay dozing and resting. She had been given an overdose of chloroform, and for a little while it had been touch-and-go. Now she and the baby were both out of danger, and the child, born January 30, 1882, was resting as quietly as his mother.

Mr. Roosevelt sat down to enter in his wife's diary:

"At quarter to nine my Sallie had a splendid large baby boy. He weighs ten pounds without clothes."

To the home of "Rosy," his son by a former marriage, he wrote on a Western Union blank, "Sallie has a bouncing boy . . . she has had a very hard time."

The message did not go as a telegram, for "Rosy," or James Roosevelt Roosevelt, lived on property adjoining at the southern side. The doctor dropped off the note at the other Roosevelt house on his way back to Poughkeepsie.

The baby's mother, Sara Delano, was James Roosevelt's second wife. She was only twenty-seven years old, about the same age as her stepson "Rosy." James Roosevelt himself was fifty-four, and he wondered how much of this second son's life he would be permitted to guide.

Winter began to give way to spring; the snow began to melt from the ground; the last uneven slabs of ice to float down the Hudson; and Sara Delano Roosevelt was up and about, giving hours of attention to her first—and only—child.

"Baby is so plump, pink and nice," she would say, and insisted on bathing and dressing him herself, even though a baby's nurse had come into the household permanently and there were other servants to help.

The parents' first choice of a name was to call him Warren after Sara Roosevelt's father, but when they consulted her brother Warren Delano, who had lost his own son recently, another Warren, he wrote to them, "I could

not bear it if you named your son after Father. He would
be a constant reminder to me of my late son."

While they were disappointed, they were not surprised; and, of course, they changed their plans, at last
deciding to name the boy Franklin Delano after Sara's
father's brother. When Franklin was seven weeks old,
they dressed him in a long white fragile gown, decorated
with fine embroidery and delicate buttons, and drove
with him in their big open victoria to the chapel of St.
James' Church in Hyde Park to have him christened in
the Episcopal faith.

The rural roads were muddy in March, but the three-
mile trip along the Albany Post Road to the little church
with its tall front steeple was a short one; and so was the
ceremony. The victoria soon turned back into the long
driveway of "Springwood," and discharged its passengers
at the porch that ran along the whole eastern and southern sides of the house. The christening party filled the
rooms with its gay chatter and laughter.

"Maybe he will be President some day," said Franklin's
father.

"Oh, no!" protested his mother. "I would never want
him to be in public life."

Between his doting mother and his nurse, Franklin had
as much loving care and attention as a child could possibly need. By the time he was five the real boy in him
began to protest against so much protection and against
the pretty dresses and long blond curls he had to wear.

Eventually Mrs. Roosevelt had to give in. Choking back her tears, she cut off his curls and let him wear trousers. For a while she compensated herself by dressing him in Scottish kilts and velvet suits with ruffled silk shirts, but his blue eyes soon flashed fire. He wanted to dress like a sailor! He loved boats!

His fondness for boats came quite naturally. His great-grandfather Delano had owned a fleet of sailing vessels that plied the China trade out of New Bedford, Massachusetts, and his mother had gone to China on a sailing vessel when she was only eight. It had been a four months' journey round Cape of Good Hope, and when she told her son the story her eyes still sparkled with the excitement she had felt as a child.

In the attic at "Springwood" Franklin found an old sea chest of his grandfather's, containing an 1812 sailor hat, a model ship, old log books, a brass cannon; and, best of all, the inside of the chest smelled of the mustiness of years and years at sea.

He began very early to fashion sailing boats of his own, and each one that he made was more seaworthy than its predecessor. Carefully he carried them with him and sailed them on the shores of Passamaquoddy Bay when his family moved to their summer home each year. The journey was by train to Eastport, Maine, and across the water to Campobello Island. The older Franklin grew the more he enjoyed his vacations there. He liked to seek out the companionship of old native residents on the historic Canadian island to hear them tell hair-raising legends of the region, tales of storms and shipwrecks and pirates.

His best out-of-door companion was his father, who loved ships and boats as much as Franklin. Sometimes they designed toy boats together. Sometimes James Roosevelt took his son out on the bay in a real sailboat, their *Half Moon*, a fifty-one-foot yacht, and taught him how to handle her.

But it was at Hyde Park that father and son found more things to do together: skating, tobogganing, and iceboating in the winter; fishing and hunting in the summer. "Springwood" was really a farm, and James Roosevelt was a country squire who believed that his son should learn from his father how to handle the estate he would some day inherit. Together they inspected the vegetable gardens, the fruit trees, the big square rose garden surrounded by hemlock hedge, the greenhouses, the horses in the stables, the carriage house.

His mother was his indoor companion. An exceptionally cultured person with musical talent, she played and sang for Franklin, or read to him in the evening, took care of him when he came down with one childhood illness or another. Like his father, she shared with him the problems of administering a large house with a staff of servants. He must learn this, too.

The Roosevelts were liked by their neighbors and got on well with them. The next house to the north was the

Newbolds' which stood closer to the road than the river, and above that came the Rogers'. There were four Rogers boys and two girls; Edmund Rogers and Franklin became friends very early because they were about the same age. One of their first projects together was to build a house high up in one of the big old trees and call it a ship, declaring that they were going to sail to China and Borneo. The next ship that they built together was actually a raft, because fishing from the bank had grown too tame and they must put out into deeper waters. They worked hard, chopping down the young trees and binding them securely together. But when they moved their creation out into a nearby cove and climbed aboard, it sank to the bottom with a few quick gurgles, and they were standing in water to their waists. They had thought that all timber would float with or without cargo.

Except for the Rogers boys Franklin's boyhood companions were adults for the most part, a big majority of them relatives, and he didn't even attend formal school until he was fourteen, since it was the custom of the well-to-do families in that region to engage tutors at home.

Once in a while a houseful of visiting relatives would include some children. His godfather, Elliott Roosevelt, for instance, had a daughter nearly three years younger than Franklin, and when she came to the house Franklin liked to get down on all fours and play horse while she rode astride his back. Her name was Eleanor.

There were so many Roosevelts and Delanos that

Franklin was often confused about his exact relationships. "What number of cousin is Eleanor?" he asked. "You are fifth cousins once removed," he was told.

Whether the young people were neighbors or visiting relatives, Franklin was always the recognized leader in the group, and a tendency to order his companions around grew so strong that his mother rebuked him for it.

"My son, don't give the orders all of the time. Let the other boy give them sometimes."

"Mummie, if I didn't give the orders, nothing would happen."

Franklin was indulged up to a point, but his parents were on the alert for bad traits that needed correcting. Some of their relatives even felt—and said—that his parents were too strict with him, but Sara and James Roosevelt knew in their hearts that they must guard against the temptation to spoil an only child.

He disliked losing at cards, his mother noticed, and one evening when she was playing the game of Old Maid with him and he found himself the loser, his anger mounted and teasing made him tempestuous. Another day, playing Steeplechase with her, her toy horse won, and he grew angry. She promptly picked the game from the table and declared she would never play with him again until he learned how to lose. It was an appropriate punishment, because he liked the game.

Franklin's formal education had begun early, while he was still in curls and dresses, and often his governess or tutor was of European background so that he could learn another language, usually French or German. In another few years he was following a strict school schedule: up at seven, breakfast at eight, lessons from nine to twelve, outdoors for an hour, luncheon, lessons again until four. Not nearly enough freedom for a boy with so much energy as he. He began to grow somber, sullen, depressed, until his mother sat down with him and tried to find out what the matter was.

Was he unhappy?

"Yes, I am unhappy."

What was he unhappy for?

"Oh, for freedom!" he declared passionately.

Next morning it was apparent that his parents had had a conference, because they announced that today there would be no rules. He could do as he pleased.

Free to do as he pleased! He hurried into his jacket and cap and darted out of the door, down the long hill to the river, along the river bank, up another hill through the woods. He listened to the bird calls, followed them cautiously to identify the birds. Free to do as he pleased! He need not even report for meals until he felt hungry. He wished for the company of one of the Rogers boys, but they were held prisoners by their own tutor. He'd tell them tonight about the new joy he was finding in life, about his wonderful and understanding parents.

The woods felt chilly as the sun passed its zenith. He

grew tired, but he roamed on. Freedom was freedom, and he had to make the most of it.

Fatigue overcame him at last, and longing for the snug warmth of the crackling fireplace in the parlor where the family often gathered he trudged homeward. He still had his freedom, he discovered. No one asked him where he had been; no one gave him any direction. He felt dirty and so he decided he had better wash. He felt hungry, too, and so he asked for something to eat. His head began to nod over his plate, and even though it was not yet his official bedtime he decided to go to bed. Next morning after breakfast, even though his freedom had not been suspended, he climbed the stairs to the Tower Room and sat down at the small round table opposite his teacher.

At one end of the house there was a square wing that rose like a tower, a story taller than the rest of the house, and its top floor room was his for lessons and games and the hoarding of treasures.

The solitary lessons in the Tower Room gave way to group study when Franklin was about ten. For two winters he and Edmund and two sons of the rector of St. James' Church studied with one tutor. They gathered in a circular room of one of the corner turrets of the Rogers house, a huge old gray stone building.

Franklin enjoyed his studies; he was quick and keen, reading far more than his assignments. His father had a huge library, and he was permitted to read anything he wished. He particularly liked geography and history, especially naval history. His well-to-do parents gave him an opportunity to explore every possible talent, and for a while he suffered through piano and drawing lessons, but it soon became apparent that he had no bent for the arts.

He was the active, out-of-doors type; he loved skating on the Rogers' pond in the winter, riding his Welsh pony, Debby, or tramping through the woods with his red setter, Marksman, in the summer. The wild birds and all their characteristics had long ago begun to fascinate him, and with the encouragement of his father he was becoming quite an expert at identifying them. More and more books on bird life were beginning to appear in his own library.

He nearly burst with joy when, on his eleventh birthday, his father gave him his first hunting rifle. Now he must learn to use it and care for it safely and expertly; he must become the best marksman in Hyde Park; he must trek through the woods for long miles. He knew what he wanted to do! He would begin his own bird museum.

"I shall need some space in one of the bookcases in the downstairs hall for my mounted specimens, if you don't mind," he told his parents, and they assured him that space would be available.

Off he went on his bird hunting. He brought down a crow, a robin, a woodpecker, the larger, clumsier birds that were easy for a beginning gunman to hit. But when he sat down to the task of cleaning, stuffing, and mounting that first crow, his skill was not up to it, and neither was his stomach. Well, then, why not assign that part of the task to the man best qualified for it? He knew practically everyone in the region, and among his acquaintances was a taxidermist.

"That's a fine gun," said the man, when Franklin appeared in his shop. "Are you going to shoot every bird you see?"

"Oh, no!" protested the boy. "I want only one of a kind, and I shall never kill a bird during nesting time."

Their friendship grew rapidly as Franklin brought one bird after another to be mounted—an oriole, a heron, a hawk—and carefully carried them home to place them in the glass-fronted case in the hall.

His collection grew, and so did his interest. Wherever he went he wanted to know about the local bird life, even in foreign countries. Since his family sometimes traveled in Europe on their vacations, Franklin had many opportunities for bird walks and visits to natural history museums in other countries. If he learned that some local citizen had his own private mounted collection, he usually managed to charm his way in to see it.

The Roosevelts were a prominent family; they had many friends among prominent families at home and abroad; and Franklin fell easily into their pattern.

All of his relatives traveled almost everywhere on

the globe, and the mail coming in to Hyde Park was full of curious and interesting stamps. He began to be interested in stamps, and soon he had another lifetime hobby.

His parents agreed that they had never known anyone who had so many ways to enjoy life as Franklin, with or without companionship: people, birds, animals, fish, boats, stamps, books, games. It meant that he always had something interesting to tell people. Conversations with Franklin were never dull. As he reached his early adolescent years he grew more amiable, friendly, self-reliant, sociable, and generally charming.

"I hope he doesn't become too conceited," his father reflected.

"He's very handsome, James," said his mother, "and he's reaching an age when girls are beginning to notice him. They will never let you cure him of that."

The fact that his cousin, Theodore Roosevelt, was becoming so prominent in public life did not contribute any modesty to Franklin's personality. Cousin Teddy had already been a member of the New York State Legislature, a Republican candidate for Mayor of New York City, and by the time Franklin was thirteen Cousin Teddy had completed six years as United States Civil Service Commissioner in Washington and was appointed Police Commissioner of New York City.

But the conceit that worried his father did not seem to harm Franklin's social life. As his mother had remarked, girls were beginning to notice him, and he was beginning to appreciate their company. Mary Newbold who lived nearby was proving to be a good companion with whom to go cycling or canoeing on the Hudson and a real challenge to him on the lawn tennis court in back of her house.

Eleanor—Anna Eleanor Roosevelt—the cousin who had ridden on his back when they were both small, had moved to the Hudson River Valley to live with her Grandmother Hall about twenty miles up the Hudson near Tivoli. This became necessary because her mother had died when Eleanor was eight and her father died when she was ten. The Halls were old Valley folk, too, and they were important in New York City society as well.

Thus, all the people closest to Franklin Roosevelt were Hudson River residents, tracing their ancestry back to colonial times. James Roosevelt's ancestors had been Dutch settlers in New York City and Franklin's great-grandfather had moved to the Hyde Park region in 1760. Sara Delano Roosevelt's ancestors had landed in Plymouth a year after the *Mayflower*. Her father, after making his fortune in the clipper trade, had bought his house, Algonac, on the other side of the Hudson, about twenty miles below Hyde Park, when Sara was a small child. So, the Hyde Park house was midway between the Delanos and the Halls.

But in spite of the fact that the Halls were less than a day's carriage drive away, Franklin and Eleanor almost never saw each other during their growing years, chiefly because they were pursuing different plans for their educations. When Eleanor reached her teens, she was sent to a school in England for three years. When Franklin was fourteen, he was sent to Groton, a boys' boarding school in Massachusetts.

By that time Franklin had grown quite tall, and all of his outdoor activities had given him a splendid figure and a glowing healthy color. How much time would he have to spend indoors at Groton? He had no idea, because this was the first time in his life that he would attend school and live apart from his parents, the first time that he would have strangers as companions. No longer would he be able to announce that he disliked an instructor and watch the instructor disappear from his life. The fact that Edmund Rogers was going to Groton at the same time did help some.

What worried his parents was a streak of shyness in his personality. So many of his growing years had been spent with adult friends and relatives, who had sufficient social training and experience in putting others at their ease, that he might find the society of boys his own age suddenly less kind, even cruel.

Franklin wondered whether the birds in Massachusetts were very different from the birds of the Hudson River Valley, and he looked wistfully at the mounted collection he would have to leave behind. Oh, well, he could come home on holidays.

Chapter Two

School Boy

NOBODY FELT CASUAL about Franklin's first going away from home. A very sober-faced party of six set out on a gray September day in 1896—carriage polished, horses groomed—to drive to the railway station. There they took the train to Albany and then the Boston and Albany Railroad to Ayer Junction, Massachusetts. There were Mr. and Mrs. Rogers and Edmund and Mr. and Mrs. Roosevelt and Franklin.

Groton School, the boys were assured once more, was one of the finest in America for boys with college in mind.

College for Franklin meant Harvard. He and his father had reached an agreement on that. Not only was Harvard the oldest college in the United States, but many Roosevelt names were sprinkled through the roster of students. Franklin's father had studied law at Harvard; Cousin Teddy was a Harvard man.

As a matter of fact, there was a Roosevelt waiting for Franklin at Groton: his half-brother Rosy's son, Taddy. Franklin was to have a nephew older than himself as an upper-classman. That was going to take a bit of doing.

To ease the break from home there were relatives and friends of the family in Massachusetts. The old homestead at Fairhaven, Massachusetts, still belonged to the Delanos. Mr. and Mrs. James Lawrence, who with Mr. Lawrence's brother had donated the land for Groton School, had a home very near the school, and they were friends with the Roosevelts.

Franklin's first glimpse of Groton School sent a quick ping of excitement through his heart. It was like a college campus; colonial style red brick buildings stood facing inward around a wide green lawn. The chapel of gray stone that stood on the eastern side reminded him of Gothic buildings he had seen in Europe, especially in England, and its tall, square, pinnacled tower looked like Magdalen Tower at Oxford University. This was logical, since the Episcopal Church in America corresponded to the Church of England, and Groton was an Episcopal Church school.

On the northern side stood Brooks House, a dormitory, and facing it on the southern side was the second dormitory called Hundred House because it housed a hundred boys. On the western end of the campus was the school house. There were other buildings, but he'd identify them later.

The school stood on one of the low rolling hills that stretched out all around them, covered with trees, trees, trees. How many birds lived hidden in those miles of woodland, and how much time would he dare to spend tracking after them? How deep would the snow be here in the winter? How many winter birds? How far away was the Nashua River, and could he hope for any boating or skating?

As he and his party entered the Headmaster's office, the bell in the chapel tower chimed the quarter hour, and when he looked up at his Headmaster—the man who was going to have as much authority over him as his father—his excitement changed to tension. The Reverend Endicott Peabody was a tall, heavy man who looked as though he could make first string on any football team. When he spoke or gave an order, he gave it only once and meant it. Mrs. Peabody on the other hand was warm and sympathetic and did her best to comfort both parents and newly arriving students.

Endicott Peabody had been educated in England, and when he returned home to Massachusetts to found Groton School he planned it like an English boys' school, calling the terms "forms" and instead of student government having a system of "prefects." In each class he selected a few students for the reward and honor of supervising the others, and the highest rank was to be chosen senior prefect.

After the parents had inspected their boys' quarters

they said their goodbyes and drove away. This was the first time that Franklin and Edmund had been truly separated from their families, but not a lip trembled.

Franklin's room was called a "cubicle" and rightly so, because it was about six feet wide and nine feet long, containing a narrow bed, a chest of drawers, and a chair. The door was a curtain, and his clothes closet was a row of hooks on the wall. Even though he was beginning as a third-former, the full course at Groton being six years, his first room was in Hundred House, the "kid dorm."

His program was strict. He had to be up, take a cold shower, and be dressed and ready for breakfast by 7:30. After breakfast he filed with the other boys to chapel for worship. Classes began at 8:30, were interrupted for luncheon, and the late afternoon was spent on the athletic field. The boys *dressed* for dinner, from their stiff collars down to their black evening slippers. This was an exclusive and expensive school, and part of its responsibility was to make gentlemen out of the students. After dinner they had a study period, and when that ended they cued up to say goodnight to the Headmaster and his wife and walked decorously back to their cubicles.

The first few days away at school are the hardest, and the first day the hardest of all. After a continuous, tense round of new activities, new scenes, new faces, and new duties, Franklin at last slipped into his bed and drew the covers up to his chin. Excitement gradually gave way to fatigue, but one sensation remained: hunger. He was so hungry. After the plentiful meals at home, the food at Groton seemed downright monkish in both quality and quantity, and there was no slipping down to the kitchen to cajole the servants into giving him a snack. He was not the "young master" here. What would four years of this life do to him? That night and during the days that followed he felt a deep oneness with the starving peoples of the world.

Whenever Mrs. James Lawrence invited him to visit her, he accepted because here was a chance to catch up on his eating, and he very early began to drop hints into his letters home:

"A number of boys have fruit sent them and it is kept in the fruit closet and given out three or four times a week. Could you send me some grapes or other small fruit? It would be very nice." A few days later: "Mrs. Minturn [a cousin of his father's] is here and I went to supper with her last evening; . . . the food tasted perfectly delicious after the school food. We have sausages or sausage-croquettes for the last three days, but I have managed to keep perfectly well." Of course, boxes began to come from home at once to relieve the famine and he was prompt in his thanks, "The candy and prunes are delicious and I am about halfway through them."

Mrs. Peabody, who had several children of her own, knew that all young boys are hollow, and she often invited a group to a meal in her home, sometimes even to breakfast.

Franklin and Edmund had thought that they would remain together, but their activities soon separated them. They were even assigned to different tables in the dining room. But they were in the same group for football, and they were both accepted into the school choir.

The nephew problem proved not to be so trying for Franklin as for the nephew, for while the students ragged Franklin by calling him "Uncle Frank," they ragged Taddy by calling him "Nephew Rosy."

Franklin got off to a careful, quiet start in his relationships with the other boys. In self-defense he was pleasant, amiable and sporting, and Groton quickly brought out his natural talent for meeting new people, adjusting to them quickly, and winning their friendship. Groton students had rough methods for dealing with lads who displeased them. Some were boot-boxed, or doubled up into one of the small gymnasium lockers, by upperclassmen; some were pumped, which meant being taken to the wash room and having water poured all over you and down your throat. Franklin managed to avoid these punishments.

His instructors liked him, too, because he was a good student, nearer the top than the bottom of his class. It was still September when he wrote home, "I have not had any black marks. . . . I got the best mark in Algebra yesterday morning and the day before I got the best in English Composition. . . . I like Greek." French was easy after his experience with French tutors and trips abroad. The first report card to arrive home contained a special note from Headmaster Peabody, "Very good. He strikes me as an intelligent and faithful scholar, and a good boy."

His letters home grew happier and happier as he became adjusted to Groton: "Yesterday afternoon our first eleven played the Brookline High School team, a lot of toughs, and beat them quite badly. . . . I cheered myself hoarse so that I was quite croaky at choir practice." There was time to work on his stamp collection, for which he was deeply glad. "Stamps are always acceptable." The Groton–St. Marks game in November —Groton 46, St. Marks 0—left him, "hoarse, deaf, and ready to stand on my cocoanut!"

Before going to Groton he discovered that his name spelled backwards had a most exotic sound, and a few of his first letters had been signed "Nilknarf." But now he occasionally preferred it in its Greek letters, Φρανκλιν.

December brought the dread of exams together with the deep excitement of at last being able to go home for a holiday.

When he arrived at the house at Hyde Park a few days before Christmas, he was no longer the boy who had left in September; he was a young man. As he stepped into the warmth and love and luxury—a multitude of holiday guests, fine Dresden china, a delicate bowl from China full of roses from their own greenhouse, the grandfather's clock that his parents had bought on their honeymoon in Holland, the menus pointed up with rare spices, the tree waiting to be trimmed, his red setter's wet nose— he was more poised than ever before. His parents gathered close to him, adoring and smiling, and demanded to hear every little detail that had not been in his letters. How did he find the weather there? About like Hyde Park; they'd had no snow yet, but hoped for some in January. When he mentioned an interest in the debating team, his mother protested that perhaps he was getting into too many activities.

"Really, Mama, you know that I can do a great many things. Anyway, debating is required."

"Do you go into the village of Groton often?"

"Not often. It's a two-mile walk, and the weather has been quite cold."

The holiday festivities at home swept Groton into the background for a few days, and when Franklin climbed into the railway car on January 5th he was in marvelous spirits. If the first half-year had gone so well, surely there was little to fear from the other three and a half. That same evening he was writing home to report his safe arrival and to say that some new boys were entering this term. One of them was from Chicago, a boy named Robert R. McCormick.

His table in the dining room was crowded because of the new boys, and he was beginning to want to get away from the "kid table" and sit with the older boys, "where I really belong." On a raised platform the Rector and

Mrs. Peabody and the prefects sat at the head table, and Franklin took a secret second look at the prefects perched up there like rare species of birds.

Spring half did not go as smoothly as the fall. It was still January when he was remanded to the infirmary with watery eyes and a temperature and diagnosed as a case of measles. His mother appeared at his bedside as magically as though Aladdin's lamp had been rubbed, and as soon as he was well enough for the trip she took him home to recover. He didn't return to Groton until after the middle of February, and his mother would probably not have let him go back then had she known that an epidemic of grippe—not to mention two cases of jaundice—was breaking out at the school.

The epidemic didn't touch Franklin, though, and he was soon busy corresponding with the Department of Agriculture about the birds he was seeing, and busier boning up for his first debate. His speech would take only two minutes, but he was nervous about it. Speaking before a group was something he was determined to become accustomed to, and this determined attitude was beginning to show more and more often. A strong will was developing beneath the surface charm. The subject of this debate was the Nicaraguan Canal Bill, and he was finding the political complications fascinating. When he looked at a map of Central America, and remembered his mother's experience in having to sail all the way around Cape of Good Hope to go to China, he could see how valuable a canal somewhere through the Isthmus would be to the United States.

Toward the end of March he was in another debate: Resolved, that the United States increase the navy. He was pro, strongly pro. The newly elected President McKinley was appointing Cousin Teddy as Assistant Secretary of the Navy, and Cousin Teddy was eloquent in his demands for naval preparedness. Even though Cousin Teddy was Republican, he had a lot of good ideas.

By now Franklin was signing his letters home "Franklin D. Roosevelt" and sometimes "F.D.R."

After his midterm exams he was allowed a short spring holiday with his parents in their New York City apartment in the Hotel Renaissance at Fifth Avenue and Forty-third Street. He was a little crushed by the news that they were soon going abroad. James Roosevelt was not feeling well because of a heart condition, and he and Sara Roosevelt hoped that the baths at Bad Nauheim in western Germany would help him.

"I shall feel fearfully lonely when you are abroad," Franklin told them: "but I shall expect to hear from you at least twice a week and I shall write you on Sundays and Thursdays as usual." Would they please send stamps?

All spring the letters flowed in quantity in both directions to ease the loneliness the three felt for one another. Easter at Groton was quiet, he reported, and the choir did not distinguish themselves. As spring progressed he could tell them more and more of his beloved out-of-doors. He was beginning to enjoy golf. He'd been canoeing with Taddy. Lathrop Brown had put his knee out during boxing. A real friendship between Franklin and Lathrop was developing. There was tennis, and the inevitable baseball.

Franklin liked baseball, although he had to admit he wasn't very good at it no matter how much he practiced. In fact, as his headmaster later explained, Franklin enjoyed sports but he was not heavily enough built to make first teams.

By the middle of May the weather was warm enough to permit swimming in the river, and he could look forward to his parents' return. Then they would all go out to Campobello for the summer, and he'd soon be at the helm of the *Half Moon*, skimming over the waters of the Bay of Fundy.

He'd be alone for the Fourth of July though, and so when an invitation came from Cousin Teddy's sister, Mrs. W. Sheffield Cowles, to spend the Fourth at her home on Long Island he promptly accepted. He was startled to receive a forthright "no" from his mother in Europe, and his reply was just as startling to her. He intended to visit Mrs. Cowles, or Cousin Bammie as they called her, on the Fourth. He had understood that he could make his own plans. "Please don't make any more arrangements for my future happiness," declared the independent young man.

On top of it, Cousin Teddy made a splashing, dust-raising visit to Groton School, gave the students a rousing speech on his experiences in the New York City police department, and invited Franklin to spend the Fourth of July at his home at Oyster Bay, Long Island. Franklin decided to accept both invitations and divide his holiday between the two houses.

Of course, his display of independence earned him a dressing down when his parents returned, but the air cleared when they saw his satisfactory end-of-the-year report. He stood fourth in a class of seventeen. He had flunked his Greek exam and just squeaked by in geometry, but his total average got him through.

The family reunion at the Renaissance was a happy one, and he realized that he loved his parents very deeply indeed. As Sara Roosevelt boarded their private railway car for the trip to Eastport on the Maine coast, Franklin felt a deep pride in seeing that his mother was such a stately lady, still in her early forties, still beautiful, gathering her long, full skirt with a gloved hand as she mounted the step. He felt a twinge of alarm to notice how old his father looked. James Roosevelt was only sixty-nine, but his heart condition made him seem older.

The train ride was long and tedious, and Franklin walked about restlessly. Suddenly the car gave a lurch, an iron bar came loose from somewhere overhead and gave him a nasty cut across his forehead. Mrs. Roosevelt gasped, and he cautioned her to be quiet.

"We mustn't upset Papa," he said.

"Let me dress it for you."

After she had bathed the wound and covered it with a bandage, he pulled a cap down over it and stayed out on the observation platform so that his father wouldn't see what had happened.

"Franklin, you are so thoughtful!" his mother said. "Do you remember the time at Campobello that you knocked out a tooth and tried not to tell me for fear of upsetting me?"

"I shall never be able to forget," he laughed. "This peg tooth in the front of my mouth will always be a nuisance to me."

It had been an extremely painful experience at the time. Somehow, when he was roughhousing about, a stick struck him in the mouth and snapped off a front tooth. He had done his best to bear the pain in silence.

No accidents marred the summer of 1897. The Roosevelts and their Campobello neighbors cycled, swam, sailed, hiked, and played golf. Everyone returned home with faces glowing after a summer in the brisk Canadian sea air.

Franklin had grown quite tall, and when he returned to Groton it was as a sophisticated fourth former, free of the "kid" table and the "kid" dorm, knowing how to get along, ready to take his Greek exam over again, and ready for more debating on national issues. He still felt some secret quaking about speaking before a group, and he had to accept the idea of wearing a band on his teeth to straighten them. He was dropped from the choir because his voice had changed, and the prospect of being able to speak with a virile man's voice at last was gratifying.

The big debating issue of the fall was the question of whether the United States should annex the Hawaiian Islands. Franklin was on the side that opposed their annexation, and his speech was well written and thoughtful, taking considerably more than two minutes. He disapproved of the United States' owning distant colonies that would be expensive to defend; it was a violation of the Monroe Doctrine. He would rather see the government spending the money improving the defenses of New York, Boston, and San Francisco. As for the argument that the islands would be a convenient coaling station for the American navy, "it is not generally known that Pearl Harbor, a port in one of the islands, belongs to the United States."

The air was filling with even more exciting issues during that second year at Groton. The people of Cuba had been in revolt against Spanish rule for almost three years, and the question of interference by the United States was a lively one. Careless newspapers played up the Cuban rebellion with stories of violence and bravery, some true, many of them grossly exaggerated. The United States government was striving to remain neutral, but tensions between Spain and the United States mounted steadily. Cousin Teddy in Washington, now that he was Assistant Secretary of the Navy, was campaigning for preparedness, preparedness, preparedness! But others with cooler heads and more patience were discussing the problem with Spanish diplomats, and when Spain was just about to agree to give Cuba self-government, the United States battleship, the *Maine,* anchored in Havana Harbor, was blown up. It was an outrageous disaster, killing 260 of the crew and officers. No one really knew who had done it, but all peaceable negotiations were lost in the angry protests and war fever that broke out in the United States.

Groton campus was alive with it; the boys were beside themselves with excitement.

The *Maine* had been sunk in February, 1898, and in April the United States declared war on Spain. Then the rumors really did begin to circulate, and the boys at Groton were bursting. "It is rumored," Franklin wrote home to warn his parents, "that Spain has sent a squadron of fifty or sixty ships against New York and the coast, so you may run right into them and end up in a Spanish prison!"

Congress had authorized three cavalry regiments, and the First United States Volunteer Cavalry outfit was called the "Rough Riders," many of them men who had known Cousin Teddy in his bronc-busting and ranching days out West. Soon Cousin Teddy announced that he was not going to remain in Washington during the war. He was going into battle in Cuba with his "Rough

Riders," second in command under General S. B. M. Young.

Franklin and his best friend, Lathrop Brown, talked and talked about it. They knew that men were volunteering from all over the United States. Scores of men who had been in Harvard with Cousin Teddy were applying. It was natural for a man to want to serve his country, and they were men, weren't they—he and Lathrop? Wasn't there some way that they could join up? Groton would never allow it; neither would their families.

"We're old enough."

"Of course, we are. At least we've lost our kid voices."

"We're tall enough to pass for eighteen. You look eighteen."

"So do you, maybe older."

Carefully they laid a plan of escape from the school. Once away, it would be a simple matter to find the nearest recruiting office. After they were in uniform and on the battlefield what could anyone do about it?

But in gymnasium an instructor came up to them and asked about some strange colorations on their skin.

"Go to the infirmary, boys."

"We feel fine."

"Go right now."

"Right now" at Groton did not mean ten minutes from now. Franklin and Lathrop were diagnosed as two cases of scarlet fever and rushed to the isolation ward before they could start an epidemic, and that was their war service for the duration.

Once more Mrs. James Roosevelt hurried to her sick son, but she would not be allowed to see him, she was told. Not allowed to see her own son? Groton authorities began to realize from whom Franklin inherited his stubborn no-retreat temperament that lurked behind a gentle, charming exterior. Mrs. Roosevelt found a stepladder, stood it up outside of the infirmary window, and mounted to the top to have a look at her sick boy. Each day saw her perched on top of the stepladder, and since the weather was warm enough to permit the window to be opened, she always brought one of his favorite books and read to him for an hour or two. This went on until he was well enough to be taken home.

Weak and wan, Franklin and Lathrop listened to news of how General Young had been stricken with fever in Cuba and Cousin Teddy had taken command. Franklin was home in Hyde Park when Cousin Teddy landed with his outfit at Montauk Point, Long Island, victorious in the war against Spain, hero of the battle of San Juan Hill, the most popular man in America. Talk of running him for Governor of New York began to circulate almost at once. And he *was* elected Governor in November and held that office for the rest of Franklin's stay at Groton.

Franklin the fifth-former, sixteen-going-on-seventeen, was developing the kind of personality you would expect from a young man whose parents had plenty of money and connections, who was in his third year at an exclusive private school, and who now had a cousin who was Governor of New York State. In addition to the usual overconfidence that would be typical of his age, he had the unconscious habit of tilting his head upward and rather looking down at the person he was talking to.

He was doing some writing for the school paper, the *Grotonian*, and his interest in sports was shifting more and more to those that would be part of his life when he left school. His tennis was good, and his golf game was improving rapidly.

He was learning to play the mandolin so that he would be popular at parties. And there were many parties in his life, especially around the Christmas season, when all the young people were home from college. Much correspondence went on between mother and son about the holiday season of 1898–99. There were to be several dances, one in New York, another in Orange, New Jersey. For the Orange dance he had invited someone named Laura, but for the New York affair he wrote to his mother, "I wish you would think up some decent partner for me for the New York dance . . . so that I can get somebody early, and not get palmed off on some ice-cart."

It irked him a little that he still wore the band on his teeth, but that would soon be over with. His vanity about his appearance was certainly justified by what he saw in a mirror—a marked resemblance to his beautiful mother—and the adoration he could not help seeing in his parents' eyes. The servants pampered him and deferred to him all the time, and like the rest of his clan he was rapidly approaching six feet in height and would eventually pass it. Often when he received new clothes from home he had to return them with a "thank you but please send me a size larger." The fit of a gentleman's clothes really mattered, especially with the holiday season coming up; and when he appeared at the dance at the Orange Country Club, his appointments were in perfect line and fit.

There was a goodly sprinkling of Roosevelts at that dance, something to be expected, and early in the evening he noticed one that he had not seen since she was a very small girl, small enough to ride on his back: Eleanor Roosevelt, Cousin Teddy's brother's daughter. She was tall now, rather awkward, and behaved as though she had been forced to come and was trying to make herself invisible. The generous, considerate side of Franklin's nature responded, and he crossed the room and asked her to dance. Frightened and grateful, she accepted.

"I really am old enough for long skirts," she apologized, "but Grandmother makes me wear these short things."

"On this crowded dance floor it isn't noticeable," he assured her.

She, too, was wearing a band on her teeth. She must

be about fifteen now, he reckoned. She had a wealth of golden blond hair that framed her face in a soft pompadour, and big deep blue eyes. Her mouth was rather large and her chin too short, but she was certainly no ice-cart.

"I'm escaping soon," she was telling him. "Grandmother is sending me to England to acquire a polish." Then she graciously asked, "Do you like Groton?"

This launched him on his favorite monologue, proved her a good listener, and when the dance was concluded he escorted her back to where he had found her, convinced that his fifth-cousin-once-removed was charming.

The brief meeting was lost in the gaiety of the evening and the remainder of the holiday season.

The last of fifth form and the final year at Groton swept by like a river in full flood: social activities, studies, exams, debates, writing for the *Grotonian*, letters exchanged with home. Mother and son by now corresponded more like two friends than like adult and boy. She told him of her difficulties with this servant or that. When the *Half Moon* caught fire and sank, a total loss, they exchanged sympathies. He reminded her to send him the story of the Dreyfus case. She kept him up to date on his father's heart condition, and when the family went off to Europe in the spring Franklin no longer felt like a deserted child. He was an adult. Bird study had become ornithology, and stamp collecting was philately. When he did well in exams he particularly liked to report his grades to his mother, because he knew how happy it made her: B in five subjects, A's in geometry, German, and sacred studies.

Sacred studies, part of the required curriculum at Groton, brought out yet another side of Franklin's nature. His religious faith was important to him all of his life, and at Groton he responded eagerly to "responsibilities" assigned to Groton boys regarding their fellow man. Groton School had its own Missionary Society that operated a summer camp for poor boys on an island in Lake Asquam in nearby New Hampshire, and Groton boys were expected to spend a certain amount of time at the camp as counsellors and workers. Franklin awaited his turn at this task eagerly. Situations in the locality needing compassionate attention were often assigned to the boys. Franklin and a classmate once called on a Mrs. Freeman, and he wrote home of her, "She is an old coloured lady, living all alone and 84 years old. We paid our first visit to her today, right after church, and talked and gave her the latest news, for nearly an hour. We are to visit her a couple of times a week, see that she has coal, water, etc., feed her hens if they need it, and in case of a snow-storm we are to dig her out and put things ship-shape."

Franklin took to the task quite naturally, because his father had always been a responsible citizen in and around Hyde Park, serving as a school trustee, as a supporter of the Hudson River State Hospital and other charities, driving about in his carriage to call on the sick and the needy. Mr. Roosevelt was a brilliant and capable tycoon among his business associates, working with them to develop railroads, mining interests, river boat systems, and he felt the way so many of them did: that when a man has both ability and leisure as a result of his wealth he ought to assume responsibility for social welfare work.

But what really filled Franklin's mind during his last year at Groton was planning for college. Harvard University, and the town of Cambridge, although only thirty crow-flight miles away, was going to be another world, a college *man's* world. True enough, the Groton football team had played the Harvard freshmen and given them a tough time of it, but there was no getting around the fact that those who attended the game from Groton were boys and those who came from Harvard were men in attitude and appearance.

Franklin would stay in one of the expensive dormitories referred to as the Gold Coast, and very early in the winter he wrote to his mother, "Lathrop Brown and I have decided definitely to room together next year!"

In the spring he had to swallow a bit of his vanity and report, "I am writing in 'specks'! It seems so strange, and I got them this morning, a pair of spectacles and a pair of 'pince-nez.' Next time you see me you won't know me." The "specks" were something he would have to accept for the rest of his life.

When he and the other sixth formers reached the

point of final exams and graduation, they felt very blue indeed. They had thought that they wanted to escape into manhood, but suddenly looking back they loved Groton and all it had done for them.

"My darling Mama and Papa," Franklin wrote home on the 25th of June, 1900, "What a joyful yet sad day this has been. Never again will we hold recitations in the old school, and scarce a boy but wishes he were a first former again. This morning after one sacred study exam, which developed into a talk from the Rector, the sixth form went out and gathered wild flowers for over an hour to decorate the dining room. . . . At one we all went to the dining room for a spread, and after all were full, the Rector made an excellent speech. . . . I was somewhat taken aback when my name was called for the Latin Prize. I was presented with 40 volumes, the Temple Shakespeare just like yours . . . I can hardly wait to see you but feel awfully to be leaving here for good."

"I part with Franklin with reluctance," Headmaster Peabody wrote to James and Sara Roosevelt.

When eighteen-year-old Franklin Delano Roosevelt was reunited with his parents, he found them wearing forced smiles, and he wondered how well they could see, because their eyes were filmed with sentiment. Putting his arms around his mother to kiss her, he noticed that he was a whole head taller than she.

Chapter Three

College Man

HARVARD WAS as different from Groton as day from
night, or East from West, or summer from winter.
Groton had been secluded and rural; Harvard University
was just across the Charles River from Boston. At Groton
he had lived in a monkish cell; at Harvard he and Lathrop
had an expensively furnished three-room suite. At Groton
the students had to take the courses laid out for them;
at Harvard they could choose nearly all of their subjects.
At Groton every minute of their time had to be accounted
for, because they were considered too young for freedom;
at Harvard they were free, self-determining adults. Men!

"My dearest Mama and Papa, here I am in Cambridge
and in twelve hours I shall be a full registered member of
the Class of 1904," he wrote home on the 25th of September, 1900. Lathrop Brown had arrived ahead of time
to compete for the post of manager of the freshman
football team, and he had it! Franklin had his eye on

another activity. After his taste of journalism on the *Grotonian*, he intended to bend every effort to getting on the staff of *The Harvard Crimson*. There was a real newspaper with its own offices!

His courses during his freshman year—French, Latin, geology, English, history, and government—were not nearly enough to absorb all the energy and enthusiasm that he felt. A lot of doors were closed to freshmen, but he was going to knock on as many as possible. He tried out with nearly seventy others for the *Crimson* and was accepted as a candidate reporter. He began at once to trudge about the campus gathering news.

Franklin Delano Roosevelt was a striking figure as he strode by, six feet one-and-a-half inches tall, handsome, aristocratically slim, garbed in Brooks Brothers' best. He bought a derby hat and sent home for a pipe as soon as he saw that these were the marks of a Harvard man. He wouldn't smoke the pipe, he promised his family, since he was trying out for football.

But he found that his aristocratic slimness—a mere 146 pounds—disqualified him for anything but the scrub team of the freshman team, and that he would never win serious recognition in intercollegiate sports. He did make an intramural rowing team but lost interest in it by his second year. He took his recreation at his favorite games of golf and tennis.

There were many clubs on the campus that he wanted to belong to, and the most exclusive were Porcellian,

Hasty Pudding, and Fly (Alpha Delta Phi). Roosevelts had been elected to them before, but a freshman had to be patient.

There were political clubs that he could join right away, and almost on arrival at Harvard he became an active and outstanding member in—of all things—the Harvard Republican Club. His father had always been an outstanding leader of the Democratic Party in Dutchess County, but just a few weeks before Franklin entered Harvard the Republican National Convention had nominated Cousin Teddy as the Vice-Presidential candidate with William McKinley. Cousin Teddy was loved and admired by both branches of the Roosevelt family, and there was no doubt at all in Franklin's mind as he plunged into the local campaign. How he longed to be old enough to vote!

His childhood habit of ordering his playmates around because if he didn't nothing would be done was reappearing at Harvard in a more refined form—leadership. The adult atmosphere and the personal freedom at Harvard were developing his strong, aggressive, yet likeable personality, and having a cousin on the national ticket gave him the advantage of personal prominence that freshmen usually did not have.

So, with his talent for doing a great many things at once and doing all of them well, he kept up with his studies, gave hours and hours to his reporting in order to win a permanent appointment to the staff of the *Crimson,* and threw himself passionately into the Presidential campaign.

Reporting and campaigning were two parts of the same job before an election, and the big question on and off the campus was: How will the President of Harvard vote? Charles W. Eliot, President of Harvard since 1869, had made Harvard into the great university that it was by the time Franklin arrived. In 1900 President Eliot was more like a sacred legend than a man, certainly not one to be interviewed by any but the highest ranking editors of the *Crimson*.

Franklin, the foolish freshman, rushed in where upperclassmen feared to tread. Perfectly accustomed to mingling with first families at home and abroad, he blithely called on President Eliot and asked him how he intended to vote in the coming election. He got his statement and rushed back to the *Crimson* office with his scoop, and it appeared in the next issue in a big headline: "President Eliot Declares for McKinley."

On the Tuesday night before election, Republican students of Harvard and Massachusetts Institute of Technology joined together in a grand torchlight parade.

"We wore red caps and gowns and marched by classes into Boston and through all the principal streets, about eight miles in all. The crowds to see it were huge all along the route and we were dead tired at the end," he wrote home.

Home in the late fall had become the Roosevelt suite in the Renaissance Hotel in New York City, where Sara Roosevelt had taken her failing husband. Early in November she rented a cottage at Aiken, South Carolina, in the hope of taking James down there to the milder climate, but they were never able to go. In the middle of November he had another heart attack.

"Make Papa rest," Franklin pleaded.

By December he had decided to join his parents; so did his half-brother Rosy. They were all together at the Renaissance on December 8, 1900, when James Roosevelt died, at the age of seventy-two.

Mother and son had never felt closer, and before Franklin went back to Cambridge he and Mrs. Roosevelt agreed that they would sail for Europe on a heart-healing holiday as soon as his freshman year was concluded.

He returned to make up the class work he had missed, to resume his activities in Cambridge and with the Beacon Hill set in Boston, and to be told that he had made the permanent staff of the *Crimson*. In making the *Crimson* staff he had had to compete with many other fellows and win out against them. This did not make them his friends, neither did taking sides in a political campaign make everyone on the campus his friend. Life was maturing him rapidly. He was beginning to realize that a man must know what he thinks and know what side he is on. Once he has taken a side he cannot expect to find everyone on the same side with him.

He was beginning to realize something else about life at Harvard. Not all of the students could afford to live on the Gold Coast, not by a long shot. Far more lived in the old dormitory buildings on the main campus, called the Yard, and others lived off campus as cheaply as possible, spending their spare energies—the energies that Franklin spent on extracurricular activities—earning money so that they could remain at Harvard. Many of these students were splendid and likeable fellows, who did not think in terms of Porcellian or Hasty Pudding because they could not have afforded such frills even if they had qualified socially. Franklin came to know many of them in his meanderings as a *Crimson* reporter and to realize that life could be very different from the privileged, ample, and protected level to which he had been born. He shuddered a little to realize that some students had to skip meals in order to come out even financially.

His work as a reporter created a second big splash in the spring of his freshman year when he dazzled *Crimson's* readers with another scoop. Cousin Teddy, the big, breezy, warmhearted, overwhelming Vice-President of the United States, had come to Cambridge to visit in the home of Abbott Lawrence Lowell, Harvard Professor of Government, brother of Amy Lowell and relative of the late James Russell Lowell. Once more, the high-chinned, self-confident reporter, pince-nez fastened fastidiously to the bridge of his nose, picked up the telephone, called Professor Lowell's house, and asked to speak to his cousin. Theodore Roosevelt came to the phone at once. Reporter Roosevelt asked for a press interview.

Vice-President Roosevelt replied, "Of course! I can meet you immediately after Professor Lowell's class tomorrow morning. I am lecturing his class on government."

He was *what?* That detail had been kept dark, until Franklin rushed back to his office and wrote the story for the morning edition:

"Vice-President Theodore Roosevelt '80 will lecture this morning at 9 o'clock in Sanders Theatre before the class in Government 1. Mr. Roosevelt will speak about his experiences as Governor of New York."

Long before nine, hundreds were trying to crowd into Sanders to hear the talk.

Franklin reported the incident to his mother in a triumphant note, and later when they at last had the leisure aboard ship on their way to Europe, he brought her up to date on all the Harvard news that he had not had time to write about. He liked his government and economics courses best. In the fall he planned to take a full year of economics and both American and English history.

"The Harvard Union will be ready for the men by fall."

"The Harvard Union?" she wanted to know with raised eyebrows.

Life at Harvard was much too undemocratic, he told his startled, class-conscious mother, much too divided into castes. Major Henry Lee Higginson had donated the funds for the building, and Harvard Union on Quincy Street would be a club where everyone, especially freshmen with no other clubs, would be welcome, where *everyone* could hold meetings and social affairs, or read and study in the library.

"Are you joining?"

"Definitely."

"But you'll be taken into other clubs soon."

He laughed heartily and told her not to worry. Right now the sea air was in his face, and he loved the sea, boats, ships. The only fault he had to find with a passenger ship was that he could not be on the bridge or take hold of the wheel himself.

In the fall his lonely mother rented a house in Boston so that she could see him oftener, but he still wrote to her frequently in between his visits across the Charles River. One of his first letters said, "The Union was opened last night, a most impressive ceremony." His mother's mind was made a little easier by the news that he had made the Fly Club.

Mother and son still spent holidays at Hyde Park and New York City, and there were times when they attended affairs at the White House, particularly after the death of President McKinley had moved Cousin

Teddy into the role of President of the United States.

On one of their return trips to Hyde Park aboard the New York Central, near the end of Franklin's sophomore year, a casual incident occurred that proved history-making. Feeling restless, he started to walk, and as he passed through one of the coaches his thoughts were interrupted when he saw a face he thought he knew. And he did know her! It was his cousin Eleanor Roosevelt. How she had changed in three years! She was as tall as any Roosevelt, and her slim, graceful figure was garbed in an adult tailored suit with a skirt that swept the ground.

As soon as she recognized him her face lighted up with a marvelous smile and she extended a gracious hand. Gone was the fifteen-year-old clumsiness, although there was still traces of shyness. She was going home to Tivoli, her three years of European education completed.

"Mother is with me," he told her. "Do come up into the Pullman car and join us. We can chat as far as Hyde Park at least."

The rest of the trip passed quickly as they exchanged family news and Eleanor told the regal and rather frightening Mrs. Roosevelt of her three years abroad. She had attended Mlle. Souvestre's school in a London suburb and had traveled studiously on the Continent. Eleanor glowed when she spoke of Mlle. Souvestre's understanding, her intellectual interests, and her humanitarian views.

Relatives and teachers had done their best to awaken a musical side in her, Eleanor went on, but to no avail. One term her roommate was a beautiful German girl. Some of her holidays had been spent living with a French family in France to improve her French.

"My first glimpse of Paris in the early morning had been almost like a dream," she told them. "I could not remember the time when I had not wanted to see Paris."

Fortunately there was Aunt Tissie, or Mrs. Stanley Mortimer, a sister of Eleanor's mother, living in Paris at the time to make this dream completely possible.

Sara Roosevelt was most pleased by the report she was receiving on Eleanor's education. She was convinced that foreign travel and a knowledge of other languages was essential, and she was even more pleased to learn that Eleanor had traveled in Belgium, Germany, Switzerland, and Italy.

"And now everyone insists that I must 'come out.' "

"Of course," declared Franklin's mother emphatically.

Eleanor's Grandmother Hall spent most of her time in the house at Tivoli, but Eleanor planned to live with her Aunt Pussie, Edith Livingston Hall, another sister of her mother's, in a house on West Thirty-seventh Street in New York City for the winter season, so that she could be launched socially.

"You will receive some invitations from us," Franklin assured her, with a nod of approval from his mother.

That seemed to be all there was to it at the time. Franklin left Eleanor on the train at Hyde Park, and he and his mother were soon engrossed in their plans for going to Campobello. Mrs. Roosevelt wanted to sell the *Half Moon II*, a sixty-foot sailing schooner that James Roosevelt had bought the summer before he died. Franklin was glad she had not yet succeeded in finding a purchaser, because he so enjoyed taking the boat out on the bay.

When he returned to Harvard for his junior year, his schedule was loaded with his favorite subjects—history and government; and he was on the library committees of both the Fly Club and the Harvard Union, spending spare moments searching through secondhand book shops for volumes to build up their libraries. He was by then one of the editors of the *Crimson*, and during the year he was taken into the Hasty Pudding Club. Porcellian, the most exclusive of all, continued to ignore him, perhaps because he hobnobbed too much with the students in the Yard, did too much work for the more democratic Union, and generally seemed to forget his obligations to his social class.

The winter holidays took him and his mother whirling to Hyde Park, New York City, Washington, and every once in a while he met Eleanor at some affair or other. She looked stunning in formal evening gowns!

He was finding her extremely well informed on national and world affairs, so appropriate in the niece of the President, and he admired her for caring more about social welfare work than society matters.

"Granny and my aunts are alarmed that I would rather spend my time at such places as the Children's Aid Society than in 'coming out.' "

"Didn't your Grandfather Roosevelt found that group?"

"No. He was a Trustee, but he did start the clubhouses for the newsboys, and on Thanksgiving day he used to go in person and help serve their Thanksgiving dinner."

"There are a lot of have-nots in the world."

"There certainly are, Franklin, far too many living in a constant battle with starvation. Have you ever visited the section of New York City called Hell's Kitchen?"

He shook his head then, but later on he did see the slums on the lower East Side of New York City when he visited Eleanor and her class of children at the Rivington Street Settlement House. He found her teaching dancing to a group of very young girls, and they gathered around the visitor eagerly demanding to know, "Is he your feller, Miss Roosevelt?"

Franklin was overjoyed when his mother invited Eleanor to a Hyde Park party, but he took particular care not to let his true feelings show. His true feelings were growing deeper and deeper.

By the end of his junior year he had completed enough credits for his Bachelor of Arts degree and was free to leave Harvard, but his other activities held him. He was head librarian of the Fly Club; the Hasty Pudding Club had made him its librarian for the coming fall; and the *Crimson* had elected him editor-in-chief for next year. After gaining his mother's consent he returned to Harvard for a fourth year and devoted the greater part of his time and talent to doing as fine a job as possible for the *Crimson*. It was too dull a rag, he had long since decided; he was going to pep it up. He did register in a few courses in history and economics toward a master's degree, but the *Crimson* was his consuming interest.

Not his only consuming interest, though, because by now he knew he was in love with Eleanor, and he was earnestly courting her and seeing her whenever he could. She was still working at the Settlement House with her friend Jean Reid, daughter of Whitelaw Reid, who owned the *New York Tribune*, now the *Herald Tribune*. She was also working for the Consumers' League helping them investigate working conditions in department stores and dress factories. Franklin particularly admired her for it, because he knew how much shyness she had to fight to follow her convictions about reform.

He felt keen on reform himself, and now that he was editor of the *Crimson* he was in a position to crusade for some much needed reforms at Harvard. He lambasted the football team for not doing its best; he berated the student body for not supporting the players. The path leading to Harvard Union was a muddy track and ought to have a wooden walk. Many of the dormitories were outright fire traps and needed fire extinguishers and escape ladders.

Politics came in for its share of comment on his editorial page—with a new significance because he had become twenty-one the previous January, and in November he would be able to cast his first vote. He had begun to disapprove of some of Cousin Teddy's policies as President of the United States, feeling that T.R. was throwing the system a bit out of balance by trying to make the Presidency stronger than the Congress. Franklin was really returning to the party of his father's choice, and when he journeyed to Hyde Park to cast his first vote, he cast it for the Democratic ticket.

There was to be another momentous trip to Hyde Park for Thanksgiving that same November. There were always Thanksgivings at Hyde Park, but none like the one Franklin Delano Roosevelt planned this year. The most important guest was to be Eleanor. Franklin rode up on the train from New York with her and his mother.

At the first opportunity when they reached Hyde Park he broke the marvelous news to his mother, knowing how shocked she would be. He and Eleanor were in love; he had proposed marriage to her and she had accepted him. He was engaged to be married, and he wanted it to be very soon!

Mrs. Roosevelt *was* shocked and completely surprised. He was too young to marry, and Eleanor had just turned nineteen! Why, she had thought that the Quincy girl of Dedham. . . .

Carefully he reasoned with her and tried to convince her.

"Dear Mummy, you know that nothing can ever change what we have always been and always will be to each other, only now you have two children to love and to love you, and Eleanor as you know will always be a daughter to you in every true way."

When she came to know Eleanor's personality as he did. . . .

Sara Roosevelt was a lady to the core. She rallied, resumed her dignified role as charming and competent hostess of Hyde Park, and presided at the head of the Thanksgiving dinner table in her most efficient way, as plans quietly began to ferment in her mind to put off the impending marriage.

Eleanor wrote her a most humble note when she returned to New York:

"Dearest Cousin Sally, I must write and thank you for being so good to me yesterday. I know just how you feel and how hard it must be, but I do so want you to learn to love me a little. You must know that I will always try to do what you wish for I have grown to love you very dearly during the past summer. It is impossible for me to tell you how I feel toward Franklin; I can only say that my one great wish is always to prove worthy of him. . . ."

Back in the offices of the *Crimson,* Franklin wrote her another two days later:

"Dearest Mama, I know what pain I must have caused you and you know I wouldn't do it if I really could have helped it. . . . I know my mind, have known it for a long time, and know that I could never think otherwise. Result: I am the happiest man just now in the world; likewise the luckiest."

His mother in the next few weeks seemed to be yielding a bit, and at last she came forward with a very reasonable compromise. Would he and his roommate, Lathrop Brown, come with her on a Caribbean cruise for a few weeks? It would give him time to think things over. He consented, and the cruise took them to a whole list of glamorous places—Puerto Rico, Trinidad, Curaçao, and Cuba—but the long cruise among tropical islands brought him back in March still in love, still determined to marry Eleanor.

Mrs. Roosevelt next took her son to Washington to persuade some of her best connections there to appoint him as a secretary to the United States Embassy in London. Luckily, Eleanor was in Washington visiting her Aunt Bye, Mrs. William Cowles, and so all the while Mrs. Roosevelt was calling on her connections, Franklin and Eleanor were spending every precious minute together dining out and sight-seeing. When Franklin was pronounced too young for a foreign appointment, they sighed a secret happy sigh together.

There was nothing for Mrs. Roosevelt to do but accept the idea of the marriage, and she and young Eleanor strove to become friends. They went together to Harvard to witness Franklin's graduation in his black scholar's gown with its crimson frogs, and Eleanor spent her vacation with them on Campobello Island. Franklin had promised his mother that he would go on with his studies, and in the fall he began law courses at Columbia University. A formal announcement was soon made of the engagement, and the wedding was planned for the following spring.

Chapter Four

State Senator

THE WEDDING of Franklin and Eleanor Roosevelt was probably one of the most extraordinary affairs that ever happened in America. Since Eleanor was an orphan, her relative nearest to her father was her father's brother, the President of the United States; and so Theodore Roosevelt came to give the bride away. This meant hoards of policemen, F.B.I. men, plain clothes detectives and Secret Service men that the President must always have to protect him wherever he goes. Between the planning that the United States government did and the planning that Sara Roosevelt did, the bride and groom had precious little to say about the arrangements.

The ceremony and reception, on St. Patrick's Day, 1905, were held in a pair of houses on East Seventy-sixth Street, New York City, that had sliding doors between the two dining rooms that could be pushed back to make extra space. The houses belonged to a married cousin of Eleanor's and the cousin's mother.

The bride, who walked slowly in on the arm of the President, wore her Grandmother Hall's long white satin wedding gown with a train and trimmed with Brussels lace, and a choker collar of genuine pearls that was a gift from Sara Roosevelt. Lathrop Brown was best man, and the Reverend Endicott Peabody performed the ceremony.

The ceremony was in one house and refreshments were served in the other, and scarcely had the serving begun than the bride and groom had to exchange a secret smile of amusement, because they had been left completely alone and forgotten while the guests crowded around the jovial President, to listen eagerly while he told story after story of his adventures in the Wild West. He automatically stole the show wherever he went.

At last, after the wedding cake had been cut, and Eleanor had changed into traveling clothes, Mr. and Mrs. Franklin Delano Roosevelt were able to leave for a one-week honeymoon at Hyde Park. They returned to New York to live in a small apartment at the Hotel Webster on West Forty-fifth Street, and Sara Roosevelt rented a house at 200 Madison Avenue so that she could be near them. As soon as Franklin finished his classes in June they were planning to set sail for Europe on a real wedding trip—a grand tour!

It was indeed a grand tour. Franklin needed only to

have the deck of a moving ship beneath his feet to feel free, grand, in love with life, tilting his head a little higher and turning his face into the wind. The sea was as smooth as a millpond most of the way, and they had long leisurely hours during the voyage to walk and talk, to sit and talk, to learn to know each other and grow together.

Eleanor's childhood and growing up had been different from his. Her early life had been full of grief and loneliness. Her mother, Anna Hall, belonged to an important family in New York City society, and was an extremely beautiful woman. In fact, all of the Hall women were beautiful. Eleanor's mother was naturally disappointed that her first child should turn out to be such a plain little girl and made no bones about it in front of the child, but her father adored her and Eleanor knew it. Her mother called her "Granny" because she never smiled, made her feel ashamed and self-conscious; but her father showed her off to his friends. He was gay and handsome, and he was the one she turned to for warmth and affection. Her home life was disrupted when she was eight by her mother's death. She and her brother Hall were sent to their Grandmother Hall. Her younger brother Elliott had died of diphtheria at the same time as his mother. Eleanor was heartbroken to be taken away from her father, and she did not understand that he was too gay and dashing to be trusted with the bringing up of small children. Eagerly she awaited his wonderful visits to her at the Hall house on West Thirty-seventh Street in New York in the winter and the house at Tivoli on the Hudson in the summer.

Before she was ten her father died, and she was so shocked by the news that she refused to believe it for a long time. Then gradually she took refuge in a world of dreaming and imagining.

Like Franklin, she had droves of relatives on both sides of the family. Most dramatic of them was her Uncle Theodore, who kept careful track of his late brother's children, and whenever Eleanor and her brother Hall were brought out to his house on Oyster Bay he would rush out to the carriage, catch one after another up in a bear hug, and then devote his whole day to romping and playing with them on the beach.

This wedding trip was the beginning of real adult life for both Franklin and Eleanor. Now they were free to make their plans for the things they wanted to do and the places they wanted to see. They were going to have a good time and hang the cost!

They had a few responsibilities to others, though. They had to write letters home, and they had to call on their relatives. In England Eleanor looked up some of her former schoolmates, and her friend Jean Reid was in London with her parents. A Delano aunt of Franklin's was in Paris, and they paid their respects to her. But they also took in the Paris *Folies*. Eleanor was quite shocked by the skimpy costumes of the dancers, and

Franklin laughed in a most superior way and pretended to be very worldly wise about it.

From France they went to Italy and had ten wonderful days in Venice, seeing sights and riding in gondolas. They toured through town after town in Italy, then went on to Switzerland and Austria and back to Paris and London. While they were in the British Isles they did something else they wanted to do—they took a tour through Scotland, and the best part of the trip through the rolling green Lowlands was buying "Duffy," a Scottish terrier puppy, jet black, the first Scottie they ever owned.

They didn't appear back in New York until September, glowing with happiness, a Scottie on a leash. Eleanor had felt somewhat ill on the return crossing, because she was expecting her first child.

Sara Roosevelt had not been idle in their absence. She had rented a house for them at 125 East Thirty-sixth Street, a short walk from her own New York City residence, and had even furnished it and hired servants.

"Now wasn't that thoughtful of Mother," was Franklin's reaction, and he did not wonder whether his wife would have liked to select at least her own furnishings.

They settled down in their new house; Franklin returned to his law classes at Columbia; and the young and inexperienced Eleanor became very dependent upon her mother-in-law for advice and help. The baby was born on May 3, 1906, a girl named for her mother, Anna

Eleanor, and that summer Franklin and Eleanor and the baby spent their vacation at Campobello while Sara Roosevelt went to Europe. The baby bloomed and flourished in the brisk sea air, and Franklin and Eleanor even took her for an occasional short sail in the *Half Moon II*.

The second winter in New York was very much like the first. Franklin completed his law studies, passed his bar exams, and with all his connections had no trouble in the fall finding a position as clerk with a law firm, Carter, Ledyard & Milburn at 54 Wall Street.

Franklin found himself learning more about actual law and the ways in which it relates to everyday life during the next few months than he had ever learned in classrooms. Of course, a brand new inexperienced clerk had to be content with odd jobs—to the County Clerk's office to transfer a deed, to a local courtroom to handle a small claim. He began to meet all sorts of people that he had never known before, people who had never heard of Porcellian, let alone worry about getting into it, people to whom fifteen or twenty dollars was wealth, men who owned only one suit perhaps purchased in a secondhand shop, men tall and short, dark and light, washed and unwashed. Every once in a while a case brought him into touch with local politics and he caught glimpses into the corruptions of Tammany Hall. New York City politics was quite different from Harvard or Hyde Park, but it warmed his blood just the same, and it began to feel related to all the public service and social work his father had done in Hyde Park and Eleanor had done in the city.

Eleanor Roosevelt was not active in social work during the first few years of her marriage, because most of her time was taken up with having babies and caring for them. On December 23, 1907, when Franklin had been with Carter, Ledyard & Milburn only a few months, their second child was born. They were completely happy that the second was a boy, named James for his grandfather. During the first few months of his life James was not a strong baby, and so his parents did not go any farther than Campobello and Hyde Park in the spring and summer.

Meanwhile Mrs. Sara Roosevelt was busy with a project of her own. She had purchased land on East Sixty-fifth Street in Manhattan and was building a pair of houses, Numbers 47 and 49, the first for herself, the second for her son and his family. Franklin was so engrossed in his activities around New York City that he neither noticed nor cared which lady was keeping his domestic affairs in order, until they had moved into the new house in the fall.

Walking into their bedroom he found his wife sitting at her dressing table, weeping bitterly.

"What on earth is the matter?" he wanted to know.

"I don't like to live in a house that is in no way mine," she told him between sobs. "Not a thing is the way I want it."

He sat down beside her and did his best to be comforting, joked with her about being a little daft, and let it go at that. She was expecting her third child and her pregnancies always made her feel rather wretched, so perhaps that was it.

Franklin was perfectly content with his home life. He strode in and out of the house, played with Duffy and two-and-a-half-year-old Anna Eleanor, brought friends home to dinner in the evening, and zoomed out to his office each morning.

By now he was the dominant personality among the law clerks, just as he was everywhere in time, although the others thought he was not taking his law career very seriously.

"Oh, I am not going to practice law forever," he told them in a jovial, devil-may-care manner. "I may even be President some day."

With his own cousin in the post it sounded like a good joke, since he assured them that he intended to pursue it in the same way: first the State Assembly, then Assistant Secretary of the Navy, then governorship of New York, and thence the White House.

In March of 1909, the third child of Franklin and Eleanor Roosevelt was born, Franklin Delano Roosevelt, Jr. Everything went well with the whole family until all three children came down with influenza in the fall. Anna Eleanor and James recovered, but FDR's eight-month-old namesake died, and his grief-stricken parents and their friends took him to Hyde Park to be laid in the burial ground of St. James' Church. His parents were a long time recovering from the shock, because he had seemed to be such a healthy baby, and they had not been prepared to lose him.

FDR concentrated extra hard on his career and found much solace in it, and late in the winter Eleanor found her comfort in the fact that she was to have another child.

Franklin's interests had been leading him in one direction all of his life so far. From his early days at Harvard he had slowly been developing a talent for politics. He had not really been joking about running for public office, although he could not be sure of imitating Cousin Teddy's exact course. The same winter that his son died one of Franklin's law chores brought him into conversation with the Democratic Party leader of Dutchess County. One word led to another, and before long Franklin had been asked if he would consider running for the State Senate from the district that included Columbia, Putnam, and Dutchess Counties. It was one of those hopeless cases in a heavily Republican region, and whoever ran for the Senate on the Democratic ticket didn't stand a chance of winning.

Roosevelt was comfortably fixed; he could certainly afford to accept the nomination even knowing he couldn't win; and if he did this job well for his party, he could hope for a better nomination in the future. His father had said often enough that men of means and leisure and ability ought to spend their time in public service.

There was one stumbling block: the Roosevelt clan were all deeply loyal to one another in spite of being in different parties, and the potential candidate asked Theodore Roosevelt's sister in Washington, Auntie Bye, to find out how the recently retired Republican President would regard a Roosevelt running for office on the Democratic ticket. Franklin received Cousin Teddy's hearty encouragement.

And so back Franklin Delano Roosevelt went to his beloved Hudson River Valley, the corner of the world that he preferred more than any other, determined to do the best campaign job that had ever been done. With him at the Hyde Park house were his mother and his two children. Eleanor remained in New York City to await her next baby, Elliott, born September 23, 1910.

Long before Eleanor was up and around and able to attend meetings where he was speaking, his campaign was under way. The seasoned politicans were amazed at the way he plunged into it, and so were his constituents. He rented a two-cylinder Maxwell touring car plus its owner (for a driver), and with other local candidates started out on a tour of every town and village in the three counties.

His jovial spirit infected everyone. He was gay and fun-loving as well as brilliant and handsome. Not quite twenty-nine, yet he impressed the farmers with his knowledge of farm problems. He was really a farmer in this same region himself, like his father before him. The voters in their work clothes listened to him as he discussed soils, apple crops, markets, protection of the forests.

He made a lot of jokes about not being Teddy, and at one meeting a small boy said to him, "I know you're not Teddy, because you don't show your teeth."

Another time he said to his audience, "I am no orator."

"You don't have to be an orator, Roosevelt. Talk right along to us on those lines—that's what we like to hear."

He wound up his campaign with an address to a meeting in Hyde Park just before Election Day. He hadn't been an orator when he started the campaign, but by the time Election Day rolled around he was well on the road to becoming one.

The results startled even the candidate. FDR gave his Republican opponent a trouncing and ran way ahead of the other candidates on the Democratic ticket. He was the first Democratic Senator from that district in thirty-two years. The last one had been one of the Newbolds.

Mrs. Roosevelt prepared to move to a house they had rented at 248 State Street in Albany, and FDR prepared to move from his desk at 54 Wall Street to one in the Senate Chambers. Sara Roosevelt spent a few days with them to help them become settled, and the first social function in the Albany house was a New Year's Day reception for Senator Roosevelt's constituents.

Chapter Five

From Albany
to Washington

GLOWING, CONFIDENT, the new young Senator and his wife received callers for hours on New Year's Day. As he moved graciously about among his guests, the fine oval shape of his face looked somewhat like the Democratic candidate who had just been elected Governor of New Jersey, Woodrow Wilson.

The glamorous freshman Senator did not intend to be lost in the crowd in the Senate chambers, and so, following along the lines of what voters had told him they wanted, he arose with vigor to speak on the Senate floor whenever he judged it appropriate.

Almost at once a chance arose for him to move into the limelight, leading a fight against the powerful Tammany Hall machine in New York City. The term of office ended for one of the United States Senators from

66

New York State. The incumbent was a Republican, but in those days United States Senators were elected by the state legislatures. Since the majority in the New York Legislature was Democratic, nobody needed to be told that the next Senator would be a Democrat, and so the fight was within the Democratic Party: city versus country, an old, old rivalry. Tammany declared for William Sheehan, and Franklin Delano Roosevelt led the campaign for Sheehan's opponent, Edward M. Shepard.

FDR rolled up a brilliant personal victory. His party discovered him to be bold, fearless, and shrewd, only revealing his depths when he had to. Where was that amiable, easygoing fellow they had thought they elected? He deadlocked the Legislature for weeks, and before he was through Tammany yielded, and a compromise candidate was chosen. Franklin Delano Roosevelt's name was now in the national news, because politicians all over the United States kept a constant watch on what happened in the big, powerful Empire State. But his tussle with Tammany was not ended. He had merely wounded the Tiger.

This early victory, though, gave him tremendous influence in the State Senate, and he was soon crusading for conservation of the forests of the Hudson River Valley. He had loved trees for their own sakes since he was a small boy roaming among them to hunt for new kinds of birds. Over the years he had learned how vital they are to the balance of nature, how they enrich the soil with fallen leaves, how they hold the soil in place and keep the moisture in it, and by their coolness cause the clouds to drop their rain on the valley. If the lumber interests were allowed to cut all the trees, without wise selection and replanting, the rich, green, fertile valley would be turned into a barren, eroded wasteland.

He kept his secretary busy all of the time with his work and correspondence, because he made it a point to keep in touch with people all over the United States and in other countries as well. His travels and connections abroad gave him a wider concept of American and foreign affairs than many people had. In addition, he and two other attorneys, who had also worked at 54 Wall Street, formed a law partnership, Marvin, Hooker & Roosevelt, at 52 Wall Street.

He kept his households busy, too, especially the one at Albany, where he often held meetings and conferences, and where there were extra bedrooms for out-of-town visitors.

He could not help but notice that his wife enjoyed their life in Albany, and he knew it was partly because of her continuing interest in any kind of social improvement and partly because his mother had gone back to Hyde Park and New York. He and Eleanor had been married for six years, and now for the first time she was in charge of her own home. She showed plainly that she liked having guests and serving refreshments to his committee meetings, and being on her own was giving her more self-confidence than she had had before. He was pleased to realize that she was developing a taste for politics.

Franklin Delano Roosevelt loved his family with deep devotion, and he enjoyed his children more and more as they gradually grew old enough to understand. But all of his life his first love was really politics, and political insight and wisdom were proving to be his greatest gifts.

His political insight was beamed at New Jersey and Governor Wilson in 1911. Many were referring to Wilson as Presidential timber, and right after his election as governor, Wilson-for-President clubs began to spring up. Roosevelt, the ravenous reader of history books, was familiar with the five volumes of American history and many short articles that Woodrow Wilson had written. He knew that Wilson was a learned man and that his ability as an administrator was already being felt in New Jersey. But he wanted to see for himself, and so, during the winter, he made a trip to New Jersey and called on Governor Wilson.

FDR was entirely at ease among expensive furnishings and could chat calmly with prominent personages, but when he was ushered into the Governor's office he felt a sudden twinge of humility. The former president of Princeton University was apparently quite accustomed to holding his own with self-confident young men.

Sitting behind his big mahogany desk, shelves of

leather bound books behind him, Wilson spoke with the most beautiful diction FDR had ever heard. Wilson was fifty-five, but he seemed younger because he was slender. His eyes were the color of steel through his rimless pinch glasses; the bones in his prominent jaw looked like iron. He called himself a "servant," not an officer holder. He was certainly not the smiling type, and he revealed himself to be a man far greater than the governorship of a single state. The word "freedom" was filled with tremendous meanings to Mr. Wilson.

He talked of "new freedom," of freeing the government of the United States from the hands of a few and entrusting it to the people once more. "The nations hold their breath to see what this young country will do with her young unspoiled strength; we cannot help but be proud that we are strong. But what has made us strong? The toil of millions of men, the toil of men who do not boast, who are inconspicuous. . . . It is one of the glories of our land that nobody is able to predict from what family, from what region, from what race, even, the leaders of the country are going to come." And he saw America as a responsible member of the family of nations, trustworthy and strong.

FDR hurried back to New York filled with excited admiration. Wilson was a man of great perspective! He was the kind of man who would give his life for his ideals. His great dream was world peace, because he could remember war. His family had been living in Augusta,

Georgia, where his father was a minister of the First Presbyterian Church, all during the Civil War. Their churchyard had been turned into a stockade for Union prisoners. Wilson was almost nine when the war finally ended, old enough to understand and remember all that he had seen during the war: food shortages and hunger, marching troops, and people forgetting their morals.

"Wilson could be President of the United States. I think he ought to be," FDR said to one party leader after another, and many agreed with him.

While the Wilson-for-President campaign got under way all over the United States and Governor Wilson himself traveled around the country speaking to groups, Franklin Roosevelt worked with others to form the New York State Wilson Conference and endeavored to collect Wilson delegates to the coming national Democratic convention.

Almost at once FDR discovered that Tammany was opposed to Wilson, and even though he had won against Tammany on one issue the Tiger was just as strong as ever. Its influence dominated the Democratic Party in New York State. When the convention met in Baltimore in June, 1912, the New York delegation would be pledged as a unit to Governor Judson Harmon of Ohio. In the weeks before the convention Wilson's chances were not too bright. It would be touch-and-go.

FDR still passionately wanted Wilson to be nominated, and he and Eleanor rented a house in Baltimore so that he could be on hand for every minute of the sessions and the intensive planning days before the sessions began.

Roosevelt was his usual dramatic, attention-drawing self as he dashed about from one convention committee to another. He was noticed because he was tall, handsome, dynamic, and absolutely dedicated to Woodrow Wilson. When he heard that some of the editors of independent newspapers in New York State were having difficulty getting tickets to the press section, he hurried to the man in charge, Josephus Daniels, and an important and lasting friendship began. Daniels was an outstanding North Carolinian, editor of the Raleigh *News and Observer*, a national committeeman and staunch Wilson supporter. Some twenty years older than FDR, growing a little stout, a head shorter, he was completely taken by the overwhelming courage and drive of the brilliant young Senator from New York State. Convention plots brought them together again and again during that last week in June.

June meant heat and humidity in Baltimore, and the Convention Hall, packed with hundreds of people smoking cigars, cigarettes, and pipes, was sweltering. But Franklin Delano Roosevelt was in his glory; the rising tension and excitement of the meetings day after day and sometimes all night made his pulse race and his eyes shine happily. It *must* be Wilson. It *had* to be!

This was a year when the Democratic Party could win

the national election, because the Republican Party just the week before, at its convention in the Coliseum in Chicago, had split right down the middle. In fact, the Republican Convention couldn't have turned out better if the Democrats had planned it themselves. There had been a fierce struggle between the conservatives who wanted President William Howard Taft of Ohio again and the Progressives who wanted to renominate Theodore Roosevelt, who had had almost eight years in the White House before Taft. By the third day of the convention it had become clear that Taft would be chosen; and hot-tempered Cousin Teddy, beaten, walked out of the convention. Now he was talking of forming a third party of his own. Democrats joyfully hoped that he would.

As the formal sessions convened on Monday, June 24, 1912, in Baltimore, Cousin Franklin wondered whether he would really live through all the preliminaries and then finally all the nominating and seconding speeches. Nominations didn't begin until Thursday, and eight candidates were placed in the field. First came Senator Oscar Underwood of Alabama, then Champ Clark of Missouri, Speaker of the House of Representatives. Each man received a long ovation, and it looked as though the session would last all night. Not until after two o'clock in the morning did John W. Wescott of Camden, New Jersey, arise to nominate Wilson. The demonstration that followed lasted half an hour.

The convention finally got around to taking the first

ballot on Friday. Result: Clark, 440½; Wilson, 324; Harmon, 148; Underwood, 117½; and the others trailed behind. It was clearly a battle between Clark and Wilson, until one of them had two-thirds. Through nine roll calls neither candidate made much progress. Then up stood the spokesman for the New York delegation and switched that big block of votes to Clark. Tammany!

Franklin Roosevelt needed every ounce of his youth and energy now, and every speck of his political talent, and so did every other Wilson supporter. Wilson, waiting in New Jersey, wanted to withdraw his name, but his workers wouldn't hear of it. Roosevelt dashed in and out of Wilson headquarters in Baltimore, in and out of his own home there, in and out of conferences and behind-the-scenes huddles.

Eleanor Roosevelt attended some of the sessions, but she didn't understand all that was going on because so much was going on behind the scenes. FDR didn't have time then to explain it all to her, but he promised he would later.

"Since we rarely lay eyes on you anyway, and you will hardly miss our company," Eleanor at last declared, "I think I shall take the children to Campobello, and you can join us when the convention is over."

He agreed and rushed back to the hot, smoky headquarters and meeting hall, to live for days with breath almost suspended, as the tide began to turn toward Wilson. Party men in other states apparently resented

Tammany's attempt to run them. Roll call after roll call! On the twenty-sixth ballot Clark had 463½ votes and Wilson 407½ as minor candidates dropped out and ranks closed. Tammany men and Wilson workers were all working and talking hard and fast in the corridors and among the delegates. When the convention adjourned for Sunday, it looked as though both candidates would have to withdraw to end the deadlock.

But there was a slow consistent trend toward Wilson in the voting, and Clark began a decline after the fifteenth ballot. All day Monday they balloted, and on Tuesday, July 2nd, Wilson moved into the lead. On the forty-second ballot he had 494 against Clark's 420. Wilson supporters were on the verge of hysteria. After that ballot the big Illinois delegation switched to Wilson. The Virginias soon fell into line. On the forty-sixth ballot Alabama joined the Wilson bandwagon and so did Ohio. The convention went wild. Wilson now had 990 votes and was the Party's candidate for the Presidency—in a year that was made to order for a Democratic victory! One more ballot made it unanimous.

FDR was as wild with joy as everyone else, and as exhausted. They had been in session for more than a week, and he'd had almost no sleep or proper food during that time. He dashed out to a phone to send a telegram to Eleanor: WILSON NOMINATED THIS AFTERNOON ALL MY PLANS VAGUE SPLENDID TRIUMPH FRANKLIN. When FDR leaped to the dock at Campobello he was aglow with happiness. He tossed first six-year-old Anna and then four-and-a-half-year-old James into the air, and carried the nearly two-year-old Elliott on his shoulder up to the house.

He was coming up for re-election himself in November, and he was going to campaign as he had never campaigned before, he declared, because everything he did would strengthen the whole Democratic ticket in the state.

"First you are going to have a complete rest," Eleanor told him, and he could tell by the tone of her voice that she meant it.

Resting meant skimming over the Bay of Fundy in the *Half Moon II*, his hand on the tiller, thinking of the fall campaign. It meant swimming in the brisk, cold water, floating on his back and watching the clouds drift by, planning the fall campaign. It meant sitting around the dinner table over a leisurely meal in the evening, talking with his wife, his mother, and visitors, about the fall campaign.

"We must return early this year," he mused, and Eleanor agreed.

Right after their arrival back in Hyde Park, Mr. and Mrs. Roosevelt went down to check on their house in New York City. FDR had begun to feel a little under the weather, and by that evening he was really ill with a fever.

Next morning he felt downright miserable, and Mrs.

Roosevelt called a doctor who could not determine for several days what was the matter. Finally Mr. Roosevelt's affliction was diagnosed as typhoid fever. Mrs. Roosevelt, who thought she was only feeling tired from taking care of her husband, had it too. They were both seriously ill, and Mrs. Sara Roosevelt hurried down from Hyde Park to take care of them.

Eleanor Roosevelt made a quick recovery, but FDR was too seriously ill even to think of getting out of bed, let alone of doing anything on his campaign. How ironic! he fretted. And in such a year! A third party *had* split off from the Republican organization, the Progressive Party, popularly known as the Bull Moosers, and they had nominated Cousin Teddy. So there would be three major candidates in the field in November: two Republicans and one Democrat.

With a grimace, FDR accepted his fate.

"Babs, dear," he said to his wife, "do you remember that newspaper man in Albany, Louis Howe, who supported me the last time I ran for the Senate?"

She nodded. "The one who is so thin and looks like a gnome and smokes so many cigarettes?"

"Yes. I think I shall ask him to handle my campaign for me."

"Do you have the right to ask him to take such a risk?"

She was thinking of the owner of an independent paper upstate who was now bankrupt because he had taken a stand against something that the Democratic machine was doing and that he disapproved of. The machine had caused him to lose all his government legal notices which were his biggest advertising account.

Louis Howe did consent to run the campaign, however; he saw a great future in Franklin Delano Roosevelt, and Roosevelt saw a trustworthy friend in Louis Howe. Howe ran the campaign so well that FDR was re-elected to the state Senate by a comfortable majority, while Woodrow Wilson won the Presidency against Taft and Theodore Roosevelt. And there was another happy note to the election: FDR's friend from Groton and Harvard, Lathrop Brown, had been elected to Congress from the New York First Congressional District.

It all helped Senator Roosevelt make his slow and tedious recovery from typhoid, until at last he could stride about again, dash to his law office, hurry to catch a train to Albany, arise tall and straight in the Senate to speak out on some issue or other.

In March he was in Washington to witness the Presidential Inauguration, and as he dashed through the lobby of the Willard Hotel he saw Josephus Daniels. With a rush he clasped Daniels' hand.

"Your appointment as Secretary of the Navy made me happy. I congratulate you," said FDR. He knew how able a man Daniels was and how worthy he was of the award.

Secretary Daniels' reply startled him: "How would you like to come to Washington as Assistant Secretary of the Navy?"

"How would I like it?" cried FDR. "I'd like it bully well. It would please me better than anything in the world. I'd be glad to be connected with the new administration. All my life I have loved ships and have been a student of the Navy, and the assistant secretaryship is the one place, above all others, I would love to hold."

Daniels had to consult President Wilson about it, of course, and he promised that he would.

True enough, FDR had dropped some hints along the party grapevine that he would like some post in the federal government, but he hadn't really hoped to have just what he wanted, the same post that Cousin Teddy had once held.

His heart bursting with hope, he went to witness the inauguration ceremony. There they were, high on their platform before the Capitol, the outgoing President Taft, the incoming President Wilson. For safety a wide area in front of the platform was kept clear with rope barriers, but when President Wilson saw the ropes he said, "Remove the ropes and let the people in!" The crowds surged forward, right to the foot of the platform where he stood, and listened to the words of his Inaugural Address: "This is not a day of triumph; it is a day of dedication. Here muster, not the forces of party, but the forces of humanity. Men's hearts wait upon us; men's lives hang in the balance; men's hopes call upon us to say what we will do."

Chapter Six

Assistant Secretary of the Navy

THAT SAME MONTH FDR received word that the President and the United States Senate had approved his appointment and he returned to Washington to take his own oath of office.

One of the first letters of congratulation came from Teddy Roosevelt, "I was very much pleased that you were appointed. . . . I am sure you will enjoy yourself to the full as Assistant Secretary of the Navy, and that you will do capital work."

A Washington post, of course, meant a home for his whole family in the national capital, and Eleanor found herself still closer to politics as she began her new duties, entertaining and calling on the wives of Congressmen, judges, and naval officers. Lathrop Brown had moved his family to Washington, and that was very gratifying.

As Cousin Teddy had predicted, FDR began right away to do "capital work," and men much older than he began to respect his exceptional executive ability. He found that the Secretary of the Navy did the contact work, attended Cabinet meetings, conferred with the President and Congressional leaders, and the Assistant Secretary took care of the mountain of desk work.

FDR did not intend to let it go at that. There were ships in the Navy and shipyards, and he intended to become thoroughly familiar with them. So, even though the department provided him with a secretary, he wrote to Louis Howe in Albany and asked him to come to Washington as his personal secretary. Louis Howe was completely devoted to Franklin Roosevelt. He had already begun calling him "Revered Future President" and "Mr. Future President." He promptly moved to Washington and brought his wife and two children with him.

As soon as possible Roosevelt began to visit navy bases and inspect ships, and he discovered that many of the older admirals had commanded sailing vessels, since steam vessels were still rather new. He made friends with them easily when they realized how much he knew about handling sails.

He had sufficient authority to order ships to take him on inspection trips of harbors and coast lines, and one day he was aboard the destroyer, *Flusser*, cruising along the Maine coast. When they reached the narrow, shallow waters between Maine and Campobello Island, FDR stepped up and announced that he would take her through. The commander, Lieutenant William F. Halsey, Jr., felt frankly uneasy about the idea. A high speed destroyer was not a catboat. With a smile FDR ignored his alarm and took the helm, and in another few minutes Commander Halsey relaxed and was smiling, too.

Later on Halsey said: "A destroyer's bow may point directly down the channel, yet she is not necessarily on a safe course. She pivots around a point near her bridge structure, which means that two-thirds of her length is aft of the pivot, which means that her stern will swing in twice the arc of her bow. As Mr. Roosevelt made his first turn, I saw him look aft and check the swing of our stern. My worries were over; he knew his business."

When Lieutenant Harold R. Stark heard about the incident he laughed and declared, "Oh, Mr. Roosevelt is a darned good skipper."

What concerned Mr. Roosevelt most was the fact that the United States Navy was so small and inadequate. Because of all the traveling he had done, he had a deep insight into European politics. He read with anxiety of warfare going on in the Balkan region over disputed borders and territories. When he took office as Assistant Secretary of the Navy, the Turks had just been driven out of the Balkans in the First Balkan War. A Second Balkan War flared up the end of June, Bulgaria versus Serbia and Greece. It lasted only about a month, but whenever hostilities broke out among small nations, the major powers became involved.

FDR began an impetuous and impatient campaign for a bigger, more efficient Navy, and he met resistance from both the administration and the Navy. President Wilson was no sabre rattler and neither was Daniels. Both Wilson and Daniels had deep convictions about world peace. Roosevelt was stubborn; so was his chief. FDR felt that his chief was short-sighted, provincial, and he began to talk glibly about the feud between himself and Secretary Daniels. He even ridiculed him at social gatherings, called him a hillbilly. At last one of his own friends took Roosevelt to task for his bad taste.

Roosevelt accepted the rebuke. He had been getting a little too big for his britches, and he really did have a lot to learn about international relations.

He received another well-deserved rebuke from Tammany Hall shortly after that. When he had been Assistant Secretary for a little more than a year, he announced without consulting anyone—not even Eleanor—that he intended to run for the United States Senate. Secretary Daniels and Louis Howe both tried to reason with him, but he was determined to enter the Democratic primaries in September, 1914.

Seasoned old Tammany men knew just how to handle this. They put a candidate up against FDR who was so well qualified and so respected that nobody in the party could raise any real objections.

When FDR went out to Campobello to join Eleanor and the children for the summer, he said to her a little ruefully, "Louis thinks I've taken leave of my senses." She just pursed her lips and didn't reply.

For a little while that summer a family crisis swept all political cares aside. Eleanor expected her fifth child in the latter part of August, and they planned to have her regular doctor come up from New York to take care of her. But they had miscalculated the date, and late at night on August 16, 1914, she realized that her child was on the way—and no doctor. Franklin hurried into his clothes, shouted out of the window to one of his boatmen to prepare the small sailing boat, and he was soon on his way across the bay to the mainland to bring back an old friend of theirs, Dr. E. H. Bennet, of Lubec, Maine.

To complicate matters still more, it proved to be a difficult birth. Mrs. Roosevelt's labor lasted all night and all the next day. Dr. Bennet never left her side until he was sure she and the baby were both safe. On the evening of the seventeenth another boy was born, and once more the parents used the name Franklin Delano Roosevelt, Jr.

The combination of family and political pressures was beginning to tell on FDR, and his cockiness was gradually disappearing. Little crowsfeet had begun to show around his eyes. He left his wife and new son in the care of his mother and a nurse and returned to New York State for the September primary election. By now he knew in his heart that he could not win, and he did not. He was soundly trounced, because he had not consulted those wiser than himself.

He had little time to nurse his embarrassment, because world events diverted everyone's attention. Europe had been rapidly becoming an armed camp since the Second Balkan War. The militaristic regime in Germany was increasing its peacetime army to frightening proportions, and other countries were increasing their armies out of pure panic: France, Russia, Austria-Hungary. In June, 1914, the Archduke Francis Ferdinand, heir to the throne of Austria-Hungary, and his wife were traveling in one of the Balkan countries. In the city of Sarajevo, very near the Serbian border, they were assassinated. Serbia was blamed; Serbia's offer to have the case heard by the Hague Tribunal, a sort of world court, was ignored. Austria-Hungary declared war on Serbia; Russia mobilized; Germany declared war on Russia, then on France. When Germany violated Belgian neutrality by marching troops through it to invade France, Great Britain declared war on Germany.

FDR lost the last remnants of his glibness as he realized that the United States could really become involved in this war. He began to understand the grief in Wilson's eyes, the tightening of the President's lips,

Josephus Daniels' unwillingness to rattle sabres about willy-nilly. Germany's "preparedness" program had caused all of Europe to "prepare."

Franklin Delano Roosevelt now had three sons: James, nearly seven; Elliott, four; and Franklin Delano, Jr., born seventeen days after Germany's declaration of war on Russia. Would they grow up to die in the battles of some future war? Having sons did make a man pause and reflect; it made a man long for real wisdom.

In Washington the days that followed were strained and darkened by gloom and concern. FDR was glad when Eleanor was able to rejoin him in the autumn, because talking things over with her helped him to make better decisions. The wives of the young naval officers were glad to have her back, too, because she was a mother to them, ready to comfort them and give them courage if their husbands were sent into danger zones.

From the outbreak of the European war FDR had renewed his plea for preparedness, and he had been really putting pressure on Daniels. The United States Navy must be built up. If anything happened to the British fleet, the United States would be helpless.

The British Navy was powerful, and her colonies all over the world made it possible for Great Britain to help the United States ship ambulances and food relief abroad. Mr. Herbert Hoover, who was in England at the time, was given the task of distributing food to the starving war victims on the Continent. Britain also made it extremely difficult for Germany to receive shipments of war materials—for a while—but Germany had a new weapon, her U-boats. The submarine was just beginning to come into its own, and World War I was the first time it had been used on anything like a large scale. Fleets of U-boats were sent out to encircle Britain and starve her out. Soon it became known that Germany was conducting unrestricted submarine warfare; that is, attacking unarmed merchantships as well as warships. On May 7, 1915, a submarine sank the *Lusitania*, an unarmed English passenger liner, and 1200 persons perished, more than a hundred of them Americans. Public feelings that had already been rising boiled over.

While President Wilson tried to hold a rein on public emotions in America, he told Germany that she would be held accountable and demanded that she end her submarine warfare against unarmed vessels.

Roosevelt wrote the President a note of encouragement and admiration, "I want to tell you simply that you have been in my thoughts during these days and that I realize to the full all that you have had to go through— I need not repeat to you my own entire loyalty and devotion—that I hope you know. But I feel most strongly that the Nation approves and sustains your course. . . ."

"Such messages make the performance of duty worth while," President Wilson wrote back.

During these critical days FDR's understanding of Wilson's greatness and complete dedication grew deeper and deeper. He knew what it was costing Wilson in anguish to consent at last to a military preparedness program. Wilson had seen war from the inside, and he did not want any such thing to happen to America again.

Roosevelt, like most other national administrators, planned to remain in Washington all that summer, keeping in touch with his family on Campobello by mail. But on the first of July he awoke very early in the morning with intense abdominal pain, a sick stomach, and a burning forehead. He reached for the bell and his valet came running. In another few hours he was in the operating room of a hospital having his appendix removed and had to accept long idle hours convalescing. How quickly God could set aside a man's plans!

He spent most of July with his family on Campobello after all, and could not return to Washington until August.

"It is hotter 'n hinges but all goes well," he wrote to Eleanor. "Kiss the chicks and tell Elliott not to forget about his promise to learn to tell time." Two days later: "Things in the Department seem to be fairly quiet, though there is of course an immense amount of work." And still the same week: "Dearest Babs, Yesterday afternoon I moved out to the McIlhennys' for three nights as it is vastly cooler at Chevy Chase."

Chevy Chase extends across the border into Maryland, and while visiting friends there he could keep himself fit with a few rounds of golf. He enjoyed golf almost as much as sailing.

All through the fall and winter Josephus Daniels and Franklin Delano Roosevelt worked with top navy men to improve and increase America's naval strength, while world tensions grew worse. In the middle of it all FDR developed a severe sore throat, due partly to overwork, and he had to take a rest in Atlantic City. His mother looked after him this time, because Eleanor had to remain quietly at home in Washington. She was expecting her sixth child, and on March 13, 1916, John Aspinwall Roosevelt was born.

That same spring another fear was added to the fear of involvement in war: an epidemic of infantile paralysis or poliomyelitis. Polio had occurred in the United States before, but the epidemic of the summer of 1916 was the worst that had ever been experienced. It seemed to begin with a few cases in Brooklyn, New York, and then to spread through all of New York City, over Long Island, and up and down the Atlantic Coast. Terror spread with it, because nobody knew what it was. Nobody knew what kind of organism caused it or even how it traveled. Most of the cases were children under sixteen, and three-quarters of those were under five. Thousands of people with small children hurried to trains or into their cars and tried to flee to other parts of the country, and the police had to stop them. Doctors and nurses could only watch over the stricken and hope they were doing the right thing. There were nearly nine thousand cases in New York City alone, and two thousand of them died.

"Dearest Babs," FDR wrote from Washington to his wife at Campobello early in July. "The infantile paralysis in New York and vicinity is appalling."

By July 23, 1916, he told her that the weather in Washington was "near the boiling point. . . . I still hope to get off without fail Wednesday midnight, arriving Eastport Friday morning by train. . . . I am to attend the State Committee meeting in New York at noon August 4th. That means, I fear, that I must leave Campo the morning of the third or even the night before. I am so glad Wee Babs is better, and that the big ones really like the pool. A great deal of love. I long for Friday. Your devoted, F."

His brief visit to his family was reassuring. The children had their usual stomach upsets and minor ailments, but otherwise they were all in good health. Thank heaven! he thought, as he hurried back to Washington. He had not wanted to leave them, even so, but this was a Presidential year, and Woodrow Wilson must be reelected. He *must* be.

The number of new polio cases kept increasing into August before the epidemic began to subside, and FDR begged Eleanor to remain on Campobello Island with the children until all danger had passed. She did, of course, all through September into the cold weather.

She let the servants leave while there was still ferry service to the mainland, and was practically marooned because of the U-boat scare. At last in October, FDR was able to detail a navy ship and pick them up and transport them to the Hyde Park dock. Eleanor left the children at Hyde Park with their grandmother, governess, and nurse, and returned to Washington to be with Franklin.

"I feel a sense of impending disaster," she said when they were together once more in the national capital, and he nodded soberly. America must certainly be drawn into this war if it lasted much longer.

The question of getting into the war or keeping out was a big issue in the Presidential campaign. Some felt that it was America's duty to protect human freedom against might; some felt that war was wrong no matter what its purpose; some wanted the big profits that would pour into their pockets if America went to war. The many different national backgrounds in America—representing every country involved on both sides so far—complicated the picture still more. The results of the national election were close; not until the last returns were in was Woodrow Wilson sure of returning to office.

World affairs continued to build to a higher and higher pitch with both the Allies and the Central Powers trying to get the United States in on their side. President Wilson was an idealist who told Congress that he envisioned America giving the leadership in world peace by creating an international council of nations. FDR had a more militant and impatient attitude than the President, but the longer he worked under Wilson the more deeply he felt the older statesman's influence.

In February, 1917, the United States government found it necessary to break off diplomatic relations with Germany. Her unrestricted submarine warfare and other outrages still went on, in spite of everything Wilson and other international diplomats tried to do.

Knowing that the fleet was at the United States naval station at Guantánamo, Cuba, and that Secretary Daniels was away from Washington, FDR hurried to the White House.

"President Wilson, may I request your permission to bring the fleet back from Guantánamo, to send it to the Navy Yards and have it fixed up and fitted out and ready to take part in the war if we get in?"

"I am very sorry, Mr. Roosevelt, I cannot allow it."

It could be construed as an unfriendly act, Mr. Wilson explained, coming so soon after the dismissal of the German Ambassador. One more lesson in diplomacy for the future President!

In another few weeks, President Wilson went before Congress, members of the Supreme Court, and his Cabinet, tragedy and heartbreak clearly in his face, to ask for a declaration of war. In his address he described the persistent sinking of neutral vessels, even hospital ships. "Our motive will not be revenge or the victorious assertion of the physical might of the nation, but only the vindication of right, of human right, of which we are only a single champion. . . ."

Franklin and Eleanor were present to hear the war message.

"The world must be made safe for democracy. Its peace must be planted upon the tested foundations of political liberty. We have no selfish ends to serve. We desire no conquest, no dominion. . . ."

When the President had finished speaking, there was a deep silence. Those few who felt that violence can never cure violence bowed their heads, and the rest burst into loud and excited cheering.

"I went and listened breathlessly," Mrs. Roosevelt wrote later, "and returned home still half dazed by the sense of impending change."

She joined the Red Cross canteen, and Franklin sat down to collect his thoughts on paper: "No statement about American national honor and high purpose more clear or more definite . . . could be made." Then he plunged into a work program that would have killed a weaker man. One newspaper editorial called him "virile-minded, hardfisted" and expressed no surprise that his name was Roosevelt. Yet he did not antagonize people with his zeal or the work he required of them. He still had all the amiability of the Groton boy and the accept-able leadership of the Harvard man. When tough and experienced newsmen came to him trying to get information that he did not dare to release, they found themselves melting down under the warmth of his charm and going away with empty notepads. Soon everyone in Washington was saying, "If you want to get it done, go to young Roosevelt."

The United States Navy had to get into form and action at once, and it was largely to FDR's credit that she did. He went beyond that to important strategy, proposing a plan for closing the "English Channel and North Sea against submarines by mine barrage." He was convinced that he was right, and he drove hard on it with his chief, with the military strategists, with President Wilson, with the British Admiralty, until at last it was an accomplished fact. After the war it was shown to have been highly effective in protecting the British Isles against submarines.

By the end of 1917 another ambition was beginning to stir in his heart, the desire to join up. Lathrop Brown had volunteered as a private in a tank corps. Many of his Harvard classmates were in uniform. Shiploads of young men had already left for overseas, while he sat safely at his desk in Washington. Secretary of the Navy Daniels shook his head when he learned what FDR wanted to do. One of the most efficient and competent men in Washington must remain at his post until the war was over.

FDR's political associates wanted him to think about running for Governor of New York State in the fall, but he declined. The war had to come first, and after the war a lasting peace. He had seen Wilson's vision.

President Wilson presented his famous "Fourteen Points" to Congress in January, 1918, and in them he outlined a plan for his great ideal as soon as the war was finished: open treaties openly arrived at, freedom of the seas, fair trade laws, and his Fourteenth Point was the most important of all: "A general association of nations must be formed . . . for the purpose of affording mutual guarantees of political independence and territorial integrity to great and small states alike."

The administration did let Mr. Roosevelt see the war at first hand during the summer of 1918, when he was sent abroad to inspect American naval forces and to learn all he could about the combat area.

There could be no seeing him off, because of the secrecy of it all, and the destroyer that he sailed on, part of an escort to five transports, had to take a zigzag route to deceive submarines. He walked the deck, talked to other men aboard in a calm voice, trying to conceal his excitement and tension. This was what he had been sending other men out to do.

He reached England first, where he consulted British and American naval officers and visited the wounded in the hospitals. "One feels much closer to the actual fighting here," he wrote in his diary. "One of my Marine Regiments has lost 1200 and another 800 men." When he crossed the Channel to France, landing at a port town called Dunkirk, his spirits plunged downward. Dunkirk was important militarily and had had a bad time of it. "There is not a whole house left in this place . . . it has been bombed every night that flying was possible for three years . . . I did not see one pane of glass in the town, and almost every house-front is pock-marked by fragments of shell. . . ."

Slowly, steadily the real meaning of war was becoming apparent to him. He took refuge in a bomb shelter during a raid and saw the calm heroism of the people. He passed through Calais on his way to Paris. "Calais has been badly bombed." Along the roadways his official limousine passed divisions of men moving up. "All towns and villages have troops billeted in them." Paris had almost been occupied by the advancing German lines, and FDR had a feeling of being very close to the war indeed. Before setting out for the front he attended a luncheon in Paris in honor of Herbert Hoover and had an opportunity to talk to Monsieur Poincaré, President of the French Republic, and Madame Poincaré.

The road to the front was even grimmer than the road from the coast to Paris. He went through villages that had been devastated. At Château-Thierry, on the Marne River, he found "complete destruction." This had been the scene of a vital part of the Second Battle of the Marne in which the Allies had triumphed only a few days before. "In the field in front of us frequent little crosses marked the men who had fallen in the open."

Wherever Franklin Delano Roosevelt looked he saw "overturned boulders, down trees, hastily improvised shelter pits, rusty bayonets, broken guns, emergency ration tins, hand grenades, discarded overcoats, rain-stained love letters. . . ." No wonder President Wilson suffered so deeply when he asked Congress for a declaration of war! No wonder! His own conviction about world peace was growing deeper.

His motor car moved up into villages even more recently shelled, until at last they came to the "first sign of actual operations, an observation balloon." He was in a hospital watching a soldier being treated on an operating table when a shell hit their building and shattered all the window panes, and when his car passed a part of a road under surveillance by the Germans a shell exploded just behind it.

He rode over the supply route to Verdun—"not a house remains intact"—donned helmet and gas mask with his companions to visit the battlefield, and saw the troops resting in insanitary, unventilated tunnels. He went to within a few hundred yards of the firing line, saw the "ground terribly churned by shell fire . . . bare and brown and dead."

Well, he'd wanted to see war, and this was it.

This was how civilized men settled their differences.

Chapter Seven

Polio Strikes

WHEN FDR WENT ABOARD his ship at Brest, France, to return to America, he was feeling feverish and wretched, and his joints ached. Many others aboard felt the same way, because they had caught influenza from the epidemic that was rampant in Europe. In fact, many died before the ship reached New York, and Roosevelt's attack turned into pneumonia. Eleanor had to meet him at the dock with an ambulance and a doctor and take him to Hyde Park for a long illness and a slow convalescence.

It was a very trying and testing time for so active a man, particularly when he knew how he was needed in Washington. But it did give him a chance to enjoy a complete reunion with his family. They had really been so separated by world and national events! Anna Eleanor, twelve, had acquired a police puppy named Chief, and she and her father could now have a long discussion about him. Other dogs belonged to the whole family, she argued and pleaded, but this one was her very own, and she wanted to keep him on that basis. FDR allowed himself to be convinced. His sons crowded around him with the boats they had been fashioning, the bugs and beetles they had been collecting, and they could enter their pleas for hunting rifles as soon as they were old enough. Their father would take them tramping through the woods as soon as he was able, he promised, the same woods he had tramped through as a boy. But what about their *boat* at Campobello, they all wanted to know. They would have another, he assured them. He had sold the *Half Moon II* to the government, because he knew it was needed for local maneuvers.

"You will have a sailing boat," he declared happily, "and each of you will learn to handle her yourselves."

After the children were in bed Franklin and Eleanor had the time to discuss their futures, especially their education. Anna was being educated in private schools in the national capital and in New York City. In those days girls did not often plan on going to college, and Anna's parents were not planning it for her although she did eventually attend Cornell Agricultural College for a few months before her marriage.

The boys, of course, would go to Groton; their applications had been placed on file long ago. James would be the first in the fall of 1920.

There was something else that husband and wife must

discuss, something about which FDR was deeply troubled.

"Babs, as soon as I am well again, I must join up. I can't remain here while men over there suffer as I saw them suffer."

Destiny had other plans for him. No sooner had he and Eleanor and the children returned to Washington than the influenza epidemic that was still raging swept through the family. He and the children and three of the servants came down with it. Eleanor, whose capabilities had been improving by leaps and bounds in recent years, managed to take care of them all with the help of only one nurse and still continue her work for the Red Cross.

World events prevented him from joining up, too. On November 11, 1918, the war ended. Austria-Hungary had collapsed during the summer; Bulgaria and Turkey had surrendered in September; and the armistice between Germany and the Allies soon followed.

FDR knew what would come next. The United States had entered the war with nothing to gain for herself, the only country that had entered on that basis, and thinking people of the world were looking to her to create a workable peace. Woodrow Wilson was her envoy to the Paris peace treaty conference.

Early in December President Wilson and other diplomats sailed for Europe, and the following month so did the Roosevelts. As Assistant Secretary of the Navy, FDR had to go abroad to oversee the demobilization of navy material and personnel.

Franklin and Eleanor were aboard ship on their way over when they heard that Teddy Roosevelt had died, and as soon as they reached Paris they looked up two of his sons who were there, Kermit and Theodore, Jr. All four of Cousin Teddy's sons had been in the service; Archibald, Theodore, Jr., and Quentin were with the U. S. Forces, and Quentin had been killed. Kermit was with the British Army.

The Roosevelts met all sorts of important personages at social gatherings, and anybody who was anybody seemed to be arriving in Paris. Bits and pieces of news of the peace conference filtered to them. It wasn't going well. President Wilson was fighting valiantly for his League of Nations idea, but he had to realize time and again that others were there to look after their own interests and to punish Germany with territorial losses and reparations way beyond her ability to pay. The idealists who, like Wilson, were looking far into the future, had a most difficult and discouraging time of it. They did succeed, though, in getting a Covenant of a League of Nations included in the final peace treaty that was signed at Versailles outside of Paris.

Franklin and Eleanor Roosevelt returned on the same ship as President and Mrs. Wilson, and one day they were invited to join the Wilsons for luncheon. Of course,

Mr. Wilson spoke to them of the subject to which his whole soul was dedicated:

"The United States must go in or it will break the heart of the world, for she is the only nation that all feel is disinterested and all trust."

The ovation that was waiting for President Wilson when the ship docked in Boston gave the Roosevelts a thrill of hope. Their car followed his through streets lined with cheering throngs to a luncheon prepared in their honor by Governor and Mrs. Calvin Coolidge. The journey back to Washington was filled with the same kind of happy encouragement.

But after they had been home a while they realized that a severe reaction was setting in, unfavorable to any plan for involving the United States with European countries. President Wilson traveled and spoke from one end of the country to the other, explaining the League of Nations. So did FDR. But the isolationist tide kept rising.

For Wilson, the rejection of his great dream at home was heartbreaking, and toward the end of September the Roosevelts received word that President Wilson had collapsed after speaking to an audience in Pueblo, Colorado. On returning to Washington Wilson was stricken by a thrombosis that paralyzed his whole left side.

"It's up to his party to carry on the crusade for a world

organization," was FDR's opinion, and many, although not all, agreed with him.

The Democratic Party had lost control of both houses in the 1918 elections, and by the time the 1920 Presidential elections began to roll around there was a strong Republican trend in full swing throughout the country.

In June the excitements of national conventions had to be lived through again. The Republicans met in Chicago, their split healed, and nominated the conservative Senator Warren G. Harding of Ohio.

FDR went to the Democratic convention in San Francisco determined to do all he could to make the League of Nations a major plank in the platform. And he wanted Governor Alfred E. Smith of New York to have the nomination.

Al Smith's story was just the opposite of FDR's. Smith had been born into a poor Irish immigrant family in the slums of New York City, the slums that Eleanor had showed to Franklin. Smith's father had died when Al was only twelve, so he had to leave school and go to work. While his mother worked in an umbrella factory, he earned what he could as a day laborer and later he put in twelve hours a day in the Fulton Fish Market. He was a mature and seasoned fellow by the time he was twenty-one, active in district politics, and he had come up in public office the slow, hard way, learning government step by step. By the time he became a member of the state legislature he knew what reforms and improvements in the state government were needed, and when he became Governor he put many of them into effect.

FDR found the usual confusions, lobbying, pre-convention conferences and planning, when he arrived at San Francisco. The outcome was very much in doubt, just as it had been in Baltimore eight years ago. But on the opening day a huge oil painting of President Wilson was unveiled, and a demonstration burst forth in honor of the now stricken President that made FDR's heart swell to bursting—until he took a second look at the New York delegation. They had not risen to join the demonstration! Well, he'd show them whether they could control the thinking of his state! He strode into the midst of them, seized the state banner from a burly fellow, and rushed into the parade in the aisles with it, lifting it as high as he could, and he was a mighty tall man.

When the time came for nominating candidates, Franklin Delano Roosevelt was one of the speakers to second Al Smith's nomination. He had had to wait impatiently through a whole series of nominations, seconds, and demonstrations, since the states were called alphabetically, and then through another whole list. There were twenty-two candidates on the first ballot, but only four of them showed real strength: Top of the list was William G. McAdoo of California, who was President Wilson's son-in-law; next came A. Mitchell Palmer of Pennsylvania; then Governor James M. Cox of Ohio; and last was Al Smith.

Then came the balloting, balloting, balloting. Al Smith lost ground rapidly, and at last it was a contest between McAdoo and Cox. On the forty-fourth state-by-state roll call Cox finally won.

But what of the Vice-Presidency? That candidate ought to be a Wilson man, and he ought to come from a different section of the country than Cox.

"What is your preference, Mr. Cox?" the party workers asked.

"My choice is Franklin D. Roosevelt of New York," he replied.

FDR was not present at this conference behind the scenes, but when he was asked if he would be Mr. Cox's running mate, he came alive like a young horse tossing his mane and pawing the ground, eager for the race to begin.

The convention had already adopted a strong plank endorsing the League of Nations! Now Woodrow Wilson would be justified! They would campaign in every corner of the nation, and they would win—even against the turning tide!

Someone from Ohio placed his name in nomination, and beaming Governor Al Smith made the seconding speech. FDR was surprised at the ovation he received. In fact, other candidates gradually withdrew, and he was nominated by acclamation.

His acceptance speech made a splendid impression: "I accept the nomination for the office of Vice-President with humbleness and with a deep wish to give to our beloved country the best that is in me . . . we must open our eyes and see that modern civilization has become so complex and the lives of civilized men so interwoven with the lives of other men in other countries as to make it impossible to be in this world and not of it. . . . War may be 'declared'; peace cannot. It must be established by mutual consent. . . . Today we are offered a seat at the table of the family of nations to the end that smaller peoples may be truly safe to work out their own destiny. . . . The 'good old days' are gone past forever; we have no regrets. For our eyes are trained ahead—forward to better new days . . . America's opportunity is at hand. We can lead the world by a great example. . . ."

He and the wise heads of the Democratic Party knew that 1920 was a Republican year, a year of postwar reaction, but that took none of the thrill out of the great game of politics as far as FDR was concerned. The contest excited him to the hilt, win or lose, and he planned to make almost a thousand speeches.

His nearly eight years behind the scenes in the national government had seasoned and matured him as a politician. It had taught him that there must be give and take, that he must not go off half-cocked without considering the consequences, and that he must get along with all the factions in his party when he possibly could. His seconding speech for Al Smith, which he had given out of pure conviction, was easing his relationship with Tammany. That was good, really good!

Roosevelt and Cox got on well, and almost automatically they agreed that their first step in the campaign would be to call on the President and pay their respects.

Tears welled up in FDR's eyes and almost spilled over when he saw Woodrow Wilson. Withered and wasted, wrapped in a big shawl in spite of the hot summer day, he rested in an easy chair on a portico of the White House, his left arm limp and useless. He didn't even notice the men approaching.

"He is a very sick man," Governor Cox whispered to Roosevelt.

Governor Cox spoke to the President, and at the sound of his voice Wilson raised his head and replied in a low, weak voice, "Thank you for coming. I am very glad you came."

"Mr. President, we are going to be a million per cent with you, and your administration, and that means the League of Nations."

Again President Wilson spoke in his frail, sick voice, "I am very grateful."

They were looking upon a great warrior fallen in

battle, the battle to save mankind from the horrors of war.

FDR's first speaking tour of the campaign took him to the far Northwest, and two newsmen who had been covering the Navy Department went with him: Marvin McIntyre and Stephen T. Early. They would be with him for many years. Louis Howe remained in Washington to clean up naval matters. On FDR's second trip across the country Louis Howe joined the others. Roosevelt made a third trip across the country in the Presidential campaign, and this time he had still a larger group aboard the train in his special car; among them was Eleanor Roosevelt. Louis Howe had an eye for talent and he never missed a chance to use it. On this campaign he often went over Mr. Roosevelt's speeches with Mrs. Roosevelt because her ideas and criticisms were so helpful, and he taught her all he could about politics.

"I never before had spent my days going on and off platforms, listening apparently with rapt attention to much the same speech, looking pleased at seeing people no matter how tired I was or greeting complete strangers with effusion," she said.

"Louis likes you," Franklin told her, and she did her best to like Louis Howe.

"Most of these men with you think you are going to be President some day, Franklin," she told him.

Victory in this election would have placed him in a strong position to be a future candidate for the Presidency, but he and Governor Cox could not stop the isolationist reaction that was taking place in the country. The Republican ticket won in a landslide. Harding and his running mate, Calvin Coolidge, were swept into office.

Nobody knew better than Eleanor how disappointed FDR was. "I think we had better start planning our Thanksgiving Day at Hyde Park. I think we ought to make it the most wonderful day we have ever had, a real family reunion."

And it really was a treat to gather the whole clan together. Sara Roosevelt was quietly relieved that her son had escaped from the indignities of public office. And there were the five children! Anna Eleanor was now fourteen, growing pretty, her long blond hair hanging down her back, her figure slim and willowy even in a middy blouse and skirt. James, almost thirteen, came home from his first term at Groton. Elliott was ten, Franklin, Jr., six, and John was four-and-a-half.

FDR was his old jovial self in no time, and he and Mrs. Roosevelt laughed heartily together when they heard that Theodore Roosevelt, Jr., was to be the new Assistant Secretary of the Navy, the third Roosevelt to hold that post! Young Teddy had campaigned ardently for the Republican ticket, in his father's best tradition, and now he was to be rewarded.

The Democratic Roosevelts had another celebration at Hyde Park over the Christmas holiday, and then settled down in their New York City house for the rest of the winter. With the family for a few weeks after the election was a young lady named Marguerite Le Hand who had come to do temporary secretarial work and help Mr. Roosevelt catch up with his correspondence. She quickly became "Missy" to everyone. She was efficient, trustworthy, cheerful, and vivacious, with a wonderful sense of devotion.

After the election, when FDR accepted a position with the Fidelity and Deposit Company of Maryland in their New York office, she became his permanent secretary. He really was not at a loss for things to do, because he was still a member of his own law firm, now Emmett, Marvin and Roosevelt.

As spring drew near the Roosevelt family began to plan on spending a long, cool summer on Campobello Island. The children talked excitedly of their new sailboat, the *Vireo*.

Suddenly FDR was called back to Washington. The new administration had launched an ugly investigation of how the previous administration had handled navy affairs, and FDR must be present to testify and clarify. Once more, Mrs. Roosevelt took the children to Campobello to wait for him there, and he returned to the heat of the national capital.

The handsome and brilliant Franklin Delano Roosevelt, with his marvelous memory for details, made a most convincing witness. "That I committed all sorts of high crimes and misdemeanors, are nowhere supported by the evidence directly or indirectly," he said in conclusion. "The Senators cannot cite the evidence in their support. . . . This business of using the navy as a football of politics is going to stop. People everywhere are tired of partisan discussion of dead history. . . ." By the time he was through, the whole case was dropped, and on the twenty-first of July he wrote to Eleanor:

"Dearest Babs, I left Washington in awful heat yesterday. . . . I expect those boats to be all rigged and ready when I get there. . . . Kiss all the chicks and many many for you. Your devoted, F."

He was tired, thoroughly tired, eager for cool, brisk air, and for a real vacation. This was his first holiday since the war. It was the thirty-first day of July when he stood on the deck of the boat taking him to the island. The boat was slow because of poor weather and a fog, and he felt impatient to arrive.

He thought of the deep-sea fishing he intended to do, and he would take the children on a camping trip. They must plan some picnics.

He found Mrs. Howe and her children already with his family, and he assured her that Louis Howe would be out in a few days.

For the next week he and his family and guests went sailing and swimming, roamed about out-of-doors, played tennis, had long nights of rest, but he couldn't seem to get rid of his fatigue. Even teaching his children to handle the *Vireo* did not seem to help.

On the tenth of August, a clear lovely day with a fine breeze, he took Eleanor and the children for a sail. They skimmed along before the wind, each boy taking a turn at the helm. On their way back along the coast they noticed the tell-tale wisps of smoke above the trees that looked like a brush fire. This was everyone's responsibility. FDR beached the boat at once, and they hurried ashore to beat out the flames.

When the fire was out they looked at one another and laughed. They were all exhausted and hot and dirty, and their faces and clothes were streaked with black.

"We need a swim," declared FDR.

"A swim, a swim!" clamored the children, and they dashed away to a small inland lake on Campobello called Lake Glen Severn.

Mrs. Roosevelt returned to the house to wait for them and to look after dinner.

After his swim in the lake with the children, FDR still did not feel invigorated enough, and so he loped on out to the shore and took a plunge in the colder waters of the bay. Then back to the house he went at a dog trot and pounced on a pile of mail that had been delivered while they were out in the *Vireo*. Without changing out of his wet bathing suit, he sat on the front porch to read his correspondence.

A sudden chill shook him. Then another.

"I don't want to catch cold," he said to Eleanor. "I think I shall go directly to bed and get thoroughly warm."

She asked him whether he wanted supper.

"No," he replied. "I don't feel hungry. I'm just chilly."

He slid into bed and drew the covers up to his chin, trying to relax. That sail and swim and sprint across the island ought to have made him feel fine, but he was full of aches, and his stomach seemed upset even though he had eaten nothing. He dozed fitfully, waking up now and again as pains in his back and legs began to bother him. He did not want to wake Eleanor.

In the morning when Eleanor came to his bedside and laid a hand on his forehead, she said, "You have a temperature, Franklin."

"I have a great deal of pain, too, Babs. I won't be able to take the children on that camping trip that I promised them."

"Grace Howe will take them, and I shall stay here with you."

His pains grew worse, and Eleanor summoned Dr. Bennet from Lubec once more. But the doctor could not recognize the symptoms.

Paralysis began to set in and spread to FDR's legs, then to his back and arms and hands. Grace Howe sent her husband a telegram and told him to come at once.

FDR had been stricken on Wednesday evening; by Friday he could not walk at all. Louis Howe was at his side by then, and he and Dr. Bennet went back to the mainland together to find another doctor. Dr. W. W. Keen, a Philadelphia specialist, was vacationing in Bar Harbor, and he agreed to return to Campobello. It was Dr. Keen's opinion that a blood clot in the lower spinal column was causing the paralysis.

"Massage his muscles carefully every day."

Eleanor Roosevelt and Louis Howe were the only two "nurses" on the island, and they worked together around the clock to take care of the patient they both loved.

The massages were painful, and FDR held his breath and tried to endure them in silence. The doctor had said that the clot would be gradually absorbed by his system, and when he began to recover the use of his hands it seemed as though the doctor's theory was right. But soon the doctor changed his mind and thought it might be a lesion in the spinal cord, and this could be more serious. But he would eventually be *well*. Of that both doctors were certain.

When was eventually? He wanted to be up, to stride around, to swim, sail, race along the beach with his children, play golf with his neighbors, plan future campaigns with Louis Howe. How long would he have to lie here as helpless as an infant?

The devoted Howe had insisted on becoming FDR's personal secretary, and he faithfully read all letters aloud and wrote out the answers to them.

The August days slipped by slowly and grimly; FDR's

temperature persisted, so did the pain. The doctors began to suggest that perhaps the congestion in the lower part of the spine was the result of an attack of infantile paralysis.

The suggestion brought everyone up short. Eleanor insisted that a specialist be called in for consultation, and Dr. Robert W. Lovett of Boston soon arrived. He declared the affliction absolutely to be polio.

But what of his children, FDR demanded in sudden panic. His children had been exposed to the contagion! They were beyond danger, Dr. Lovett assured him, but FDR's mind would not really be at ease about them until many more weeks had passed. Look how long it had taken his own symptoms to appear!

What could he hope for in the way of recovery now that he knew what his affliction was? Eventually might be never! FDR leaned his head back against the pillow as he looked at his wife in sudden despair, and together they listened to the rest of Dr. Lovett's advice:

"Drugs, I believe, are of little or no value, and not worth giving if they impair appetite. Bromides for sleeplessness may be useful."

Massage was not good; he wanted them to stop that.

"There is nothing that can be added to the treatment," he went on, "and this is one of the hardest things to make the family understand. The use of hot baths should, I think, now be considered again, as it is really helpful and will encourage the patient, as he can do so much more under water with his legs. There is likely to be mental depression and sometimes irritability."

When they were alone, Franklin confessed his bitterness to Eleanor and saw an expression of shock and worry come into her face.

"Please break the news to my mother and the children as gently as possible," he asked her, and she nodded.

She was watching an encouraging sign: a hard, flinty expression was coming into his eyes. She had seen that expression before: when he was defying Tammany, then bucking Washington to build up the Navy, and again when he was on his way to Washington to answer the accusations in the recent investigation. FDR was not a man to be crossed, not even by a germ.

She left him, then, to write a very careful note to Sara Roosevelt, who had been in Europe all summer and was due back any day.

"Dearest Mama, Franklin has been quite ill and so can't go down to meet you on Tuesday to his great regret. . . . We are all so happy to have you home again, dear, you don't know what it means to feel you near again. . . ."

Calm and minimizing though the note was, it brought Sara Roosevelt rushing to Campobello.

Meanwhile the doctor had said that the patient was to sit up as soon as it was comfortable for him, but FDR wasn't waiting until it was easy to do.

"Let's try it now, Babs," he said in a voice that could easily have filled the Senate Chamber.

It proved an extremely painful ordeal for himself and for Eleanor and Louis Howe, who were watching. Louis Howe refused to be discouraged. He had made up his mind that FDR would recover, and he said oftener than ever that he would be President of the United States some day.

They all remained on Campobello until the middle of September, because the doctor would not allow FDR to be moved before then.

"We are planning to take you to New York," Eleanor told him. "Dr. Lovett wants to place you in Presbyterian Hospital under the care of Dr. George Draper!"

"George Draper graduated from Groton a year ahead of me," FDR said with sudden lightheartedness. "I shall like being in his care."

Louis Howe had been smoking one cigarette after another, as usual, but a lot faster than usual, because he was worried about Franklin's political career. He didn't want anyone to find out that FDR had polio, and he didn't want the newsmen, especially the photographers, to see him on a stretcher.

He announced to the family that he intended to plan FDR's transportation to New York. He cleverly arranged to have two boats leave Campobello. Then he leaked to the press the news that FDR would arrive at one pier in Eastport in his motor launch. While a crowd of reporters waited there, he took FDR ashore on his stretcher at another dock, and got him through a train window into a private railway car. The scheme worked, the way Louis Howe's political schemes usually did, and all the public saw was FDR's face in the train window, nodding and smiling.

The train ride from Maine to New York City was long, with continuous vibrations and joltings irritating the patient's back and legs, but he had seen his brief despair and pain reflected in the faces of his family and friends, and he did not want to see that happen again. He made up his mind that it would not. He never uttered another word of complaint. He must not regard himself as "sick"; his children must not be allowed to think of him as "sick" or different. The sickness part was finished, and the rest was to be his fight back to active life. If he did not recover his ability to walk, then he must learn to live with a different kind of body.

After FDR was settled, Dr. Draper told newsmen that the patient had had a mild attack of polio, that he was recovering and would not be lame permanently.

In Presbyterian Hospital his booming voice could be heard up and down the corridors, joking with the nurses and attendants, and when Eleanor brought the children to see him he was ready to wrestle and play with them. He was just as interested in their school progress and their ambitions as he ever was. He boasted about his progress to them, showed them how he was learning to haul himself up on the rings hanging over his bed, flexed the big muscles that he was developing in his arms.

Franklin at sixteen months sitting on James Roosevelt's shoulder. His best out-of-doors companion was his father.

Franklin D. Roosevelt Library

Franklin D. Roosevelt Library

Franklin D. Roosevelt with his parents. He was in his last year at Groton, and his head was filled with planning for college.

Franklin D. Roosevelt during his fourth year at Harvard. As editor of the *Crimson* he could crusade for reforms.

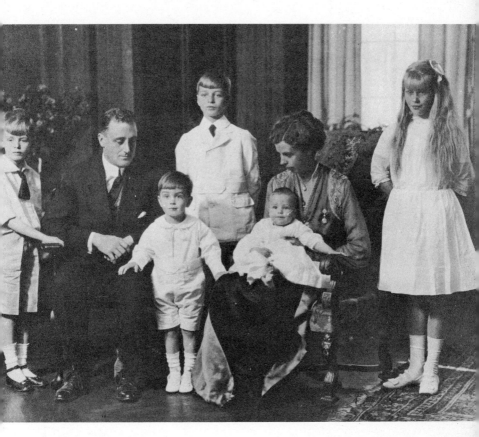

Mr. and Mrs. Franklin D. Roosevelt and their children in 1916. The infant, John, was five when FDR was stricken with polio.

Prime Minister Churchill, President Roosevelt, Marshal
Stalin: the Big Three and staffs at Yalta, 1945.

Aerial view of the plant at Warm Springs, Georgia. The
cross-shaped building in the lower right is the chapel.

His old chief Josephus Daniels came up from North Carolina to see him. Like everyone else Daniels expected to find a sick and discouraged man who needed cheering, but when he got near the bed FDR gave him a powerful blow on the chin that sent Daniels reeling. FDR roared with laughter.

"You thought you were coming to see an invalid," he said, "but I can knock you out in any bout."

The person who helped him most to keep up his courage was the tall, dignified gentlewoman who was there every day. Whenever he looked at Eleanor standing at the foot of his bed, so calm and devoted, he realized that he had married a much stronger woman than he had ever realized.

He also knew that a genteel battle was going on between her and his mother about his future. His mother wanted him to retire to Hyde Park and be an invalid country gentleman for the rest of his life. His wife knew better what was best for him. He was beginning to realize which woman was going to prove the stronger, and which one was going to win. All that a man really needed to know to keep his courage up was that his wife was fighting beside him.

After six weeks at Presbyterian he improved sufficiently so that he could sit up against a pile of pillows, but his legs were going to be useless for a long time. On the twenty-eighth of October he returned home to his family. What a difficult adjustment his entire family was making, he reflected. He must help them just as much as they were helping him. He must strive to be as able and normal as ever. Their favorite routines must be resumed: New York City house in the winter, Thanksgivings and Christmases at Hyde Park, summers at Campobello. He could sit up, and he had the full use of his arms and shoulders, and this meant that he could handle a sailboat and a fishing rod. As soon as possible he was going to begin going to his law office every day.

To this must be added therapy and special exercises to restore the limp and shrunken muscles in his legs and abdomen.

To accomplish all of these things, he was going to have to acquire a whole new personality trait, if he could, and that new trait would have to be patience.

Chapter Eight

Touching Bottom and Rising

THE DOCTORS AND NURSES who were trying to help FDR gave him his best lesson in human patience. Sometimes they shrugged their shoulders in despair at their own lack of knowledge. Naturally his interest in the subject of poliomyelitis was intense, but doctors could not tell him what they did not know themselves. Maybe he could cut through red tape in government matters, but there were no short cuts in medical research. They must work and search and hope, work and search and hope, all of their lives.

All they knew about polio, they told him, was that it was a very ancient affliction. A picture of an ancient Egyptian tomb had been found showing one figure with a withered limb. Polio was probably what had caused Sir Walter Scott's lameness. Polio was caused by a virus, a particle so small that no existing microscope was powerful enough to see it. How it was transmitted from one person or place to another no one could really say. The polio virus, once it had entered the system, attacked the nerve cells, and this was what caused the paralysis.

Only in the twentieth century was polio taking on such devastating proportions. The first epidemic in the United States had been as recent as 1894, but there had never been such a widespread epidemic as the one in 1916, the one in which Mrs. Roosevelt had kept the children out on Campobello until October.

Different doctors had different theories about the therapy needed, but there was one basic fact that they could all agree on: a muscle had to work to stay healthy or to recover its health. If its motor nerves were dead and it could no longer move of its own accord, then the limb had to be massaged or moved by some outside aid.

FDR must strengthen his back muscles by constantly hauling himself up on the contrivances that hung above his bed so that he could eventually sit up in a wheel chair. Then he must learn to balance himself on crutches.

He had scarcely begun to free himself from his bed when the muscles in the backs of his knees began to tighten and shrink, and the doctors had to place his legs in casts to prevent his knees from being drawn up permanently. Gradually and painfully the doctors stretched his tendons back to their full length by inserting wedges in the back of the cast a little deeper each day. When at last they could remove the casts, he began the struggle of wearing steel braces.

He had to lie flat on his back while the braces were placed on his legs. Then he hauled himself with assistance into a wheel chair. The vigorous Assistant Secretary of the Navy, the Wilson campaigner, the candidate for a national office, had to be lifted to his feet and taught to walk on crutches like a baby being taught to walk for the first time! After each effort he sank back into his chair, perspiration streaming down his face from the effort.

"By spring I shall be walking! You will see, you will see!"

But before spring he began to realize what a long, slow task he had ahead of himself to recover the use of his legs. It would probably take years.

Alone in his bedroom, when he had to get down on the floor and crawl in order to move about, he knew he had touched bottom in humility. Perhaps by becoming a babe again he could grow up a second time and grow better. But could he ever reappear in public life so long as he had to crawl or be borne in other people's arms like a babe? No, by heaven! If he ever appeared on a speaker's platform again, he would be standing on his own two feet. This meant that he must search out every new therapy and every new idea that doctors had for restoring shriveled and paralyzed muscles.

Dr. William McDonald in Marion, Massachusetts, was

his first therapist, and Franklin and Eleanor went to Marion every summer for several years so that FDR could learn special exercises from him.

FDR soon discovered with encouragement from Dr. Lovett that swimming was good for him, and he grew quite excited the first time that he moved his legs under water in a way that was impossible on land.

"The body is practically sustained by the water and the legs have a perfectly free motion without any weight being put on them."

The Vincent Astors, who lived a short distance north of them on the Hudson, invited FDR to use their swimming pool, and he went there often.

"The water put me where I am and the water has to bring me back," he shouted gaily to his chauffeur as he floated about.

Sunlight, he soon found, was another good muscle and nerve restorer, and he began plans for winter vacations in Florida.

As for his other activities, the list began to grow back to its old prodigious length. He darted and buzzed about the house in his wheel chair, dictating letters to Missy Le Hand, conferring with Louis Howe, planning with others the beginnings of The Woodrow Wilson Foundation to promote the ideals of world cooperation for which the former President had sacrificed his health.

The Boy Scouts had been one of FDR's favorite causes before his illness, and he decided to continue his work for them as chairman of the Greater New York group.

He and Eleanor agreed that by fall he could begin to think about returning to his law office.

"Oh, no, Franklin!" gasped his mother. "You must rest more than you do. You are attempting too much. You will overtax yourself."

It was really no wonder that she gasped, because the Roosevelt household was sometimes in a turmoil of people coming and going. Eleanor, with Louis Howe's help, was becoming more active in politics. She and Howe both felt that her activities would stimulate FDR to get back into things more and more, especially political affairs. She resumed her social welfare work, and spoke to many women's clubs. Since the passage of the Nineteenth Amendment in 1920, giving women the right to vote all over the United States, women's clubs had become more active than ever. Eleanor added still another person to the household: Malvina Thompson, her personal secretary. The two ladies had met in Red Cross work.

The Roosevelt children loved Miss Thompson immediately, renaming her "Tommy," and they loved Missy Le Hand, too. But they never could learn to like Louis Howe. He had a revolting asthmatic cough, smelled of cigarettes, never had his clothes pressed. And why should *he* have the best room in the house?

But lame though their father might be, they were

realizing that he was still head of the family. Louis Howe was FDR's best friend, and his children must accept that fact.

His lameness made him more strict with his family, if anything, and he was short-tempered when they crossed him. Elliott learned to his sorrow that it was less wise than ever to cross his father, when he protested against being sent to Groton in the fall of 1922. FDR was flabbergasted. He had a real blind spot where Groton was concerned. He had loved the school; so did James. Elliott would have to learn to love it. Emotional scenes and tears did no good; Elliott went to Groton.

None knew better than FDR himself that his personality was being changed by his affliction. His will power was turning to granite, but at the same time his depths were growing deeper and his sense of values more profound. Before polio struck him, he had been developing more democratic and universal attitudes than could ever have been expected from his upbringing, but he was entirely aware of being upper crust himself, with a patronizing be-kind-to-the-poor-and-the-sick attitude. Now, suddenly, he was one of those who needed to be helped, who had to accept help from others. He was developing a whole new viewpoint on the "have nots" of the world: those who have not food, those who have not employment, those who have not health, those who have not legs on which to walk.

His father had said that men of means and ability

ought to devote themselves to the welfare of others. As soon as he was able to return to politics—and return he certainly would—the word "devote" would have a new meaning.

Since his release from the hospital he had been keeping in touch by mail with political connections all over the United States. He wrote stirring messages on democracy and world peace and sent them to dinner parties and meetings. In fact, he succeeded in keeping his name so alive politically that the Democratic Party machine sent up some trial balloons, or rumors, that he might be asked to run for governor in 1922.

"Not this year," declared FDR when he heard about them.

This year he wanted Al Smith to run for governor of New York. With the help of Louis Howe and Eleanor, Missy and Tommy, he did a great deal to bring it about. He had the help of the Morgenthaus, too, who were old neighbors of theirs in the Hudson River Valley. FDR had made their acquaintance years ago when he was campaigning for the State Senate in his red Maxwell. Elinor Morgenthau (Mrs. Henry Morgenthau, Jr.) and Eleanor Roosevelt were close friends.

This second endorsement of Al Smith was really taming the Tammany Tiger. Al Smith won in New York State while the Republican Party swept the rest of the country, and after the smoke and excitement and dust of the November elections had cleared away, FDR fully expected the Tiger to come purring to have its fur smoothed down.

He must be fit and ready! He must exercise and swim, coax—force!—those muscles back to life and usefulness. He must conquer those crutches! His family thought he was overtaxing himself, but he knew his own strength. He had parallel bars in the yard at Hyde Park to develop his arms and shoulders, and every day he toiled along the gravel path on his crutches, striving to increase his distance a few feet at a time. "Walking" on crutches was a balancing, teetering performance of placing his crutches well ahead of him and then dragging his legs up to them —legs loaded down with nearly forty pounds of steel.

By the late fall of 1922 he had decided to return to business. There were front steps to be climbed at 52 Wall Street, where his own law firm was located, but not at the Fidelity and Deposit Company at 120 Broadway. So, he returned to the latter place, just a little more than a year after he had been stricken.

He could have used a wheel chair and had himself whisked quickly into the building, but he was determined to "walk" in that first day back. When the building attendant had opened the car door, he swung his legs out, straightened them, snap-locked the knee joints of his braces, and with the aid of his chauffeur hauled himself to a standing position and accepted his crutches.

A small crowd gathered to watch the tortured performance. Across the sidewalk and along the marble corridor FDR proceeded at a snail's pace. Each time he put his crutches ahead of him, his driver placed a foot in front of one of them to keep it from skidding.

"Isn't that Mr. Roosevelt? I didn't know he was *that* crippled," said a curiosity seeker.

Suddenly one of the crutches did skid out of control on the slippery floor, and FDR sprawled flat to a chorus of little gasps. If they expected tears or anger or embarrassment, his audience was disappointed. He sat up like a merry child tumbling in a snowbank and shouted:

"One of you young fellows give me a hand. I'm too heavy for my chauffeur."

A young man did come forward to assist him to his feet, an attractive fellow with dark hair, not very tall, though sturdy. They got into the same elevator and FDR was automatically gracious.

"My name's Roosevelt."

"Yes, I know," said the younger. "I recognized you. My name's O'Connor, Basil O'Connor. I have law offices in this building."

It was the beginning of another lifelong friendship. They saw each other more and more frequently as FDR gradually progressed from two short days a week in the office to three and four, and in a few months they were talking of forming their own law partnership: Roosevelt and O'Connor. The agreement was executed on January 1, 1925.

During those first two years of his friendship with

Basil O'Connor, FDR worked constantly on his therapy and on practicing the use of his crutches. In the early spring of 1923 he tried a vacation in Florida, taking a fishing trip aboard the *Weona II*, a rented houseboat. He returned to New York refreshed and tanned, boasting of the fish he had caught. Even though the shark-infested waters of the Caribbean had limited the swimming he could do, he was convinced that warm sun was definitely a help.

"I am going to buy a houseboat down there next winter."

His summers he divided between Marion, Massachusetts, and Hyde Park, and gradually the flabby shrunken leg muscles were coming back somewhat, but they would not obey him any more than if they were cooked macaroni, and he knew in his heart that they would never bear his weight without braces. Eleanor would have to be his legs and do his political traveling, speaking, and meeting-attending for him.

But not all of it. The Democratic National Convention was to be held in New York City at Madison Square Garden the last week of June, 1924, and he was going to be there!

What a hubbub around the house during those weeks before the 1924 Convention! Party leaders were constantly coming and going. Missy Le Hand's work was never done. Louis Howe lived in pure ecstasy, and it seemed at times as though he were happier about it all than FDR himself, because Franklin Delano Roosevelt was going to make his political comeback. He was going to stand before that vast crowd—on his own two feet —and place Al Smith's name in nomination.

Some day it would be Roosevelt's name that was placed in nomination, declared Howe passionately. Why, just a few weeks ago, he had gone into Franklin's bedroom to talk to him while he ate breakfast, and found him glowing with happiness. Roosevelt pulled back the covers to expose one foot, pointed to it, and shouted, "Look, Louis! I can wiggle my toe!"

For months and months he had struggled every day to force his will upon those limp and lifeless limbs. His back and abdominal muscles were recovering, and he was determined that his legs would too.

FDR was not only going to make the nomination speech; he had accepted the chairmanship of the New York State "Smith-for-President Campaign Committee" as well. And at the convention the platform committee was going to feel the weight of his opinion. The issues were fierce this year. The Ku Klux Klan (KKK) was a major item, and he wanted a plank in the platform denouncing the Klan and all the discrimination and prejudice it stood for. Al Smith was a devout Roman Catholic, and if the Convention would have the courage to nominate him, the voice of the party against prejudice would be doubled. Another big issue was the League of Nations, and of course he wanted the party to take a positive stand on that.

He wanted it carried to the American people in a referendum. Women's groups were pressing for an Equal Rights plank. Well, why not?

He was tingling with excitement to be in the hot center of politics once more. His son James, now as tall as his father, would be home from Groton and would go to the Convention with him as his aide.

The Republican Convention met first, as usual, this time strong and united on the crest of a Republican tide, and nominated Calvin Coolidge of Massachusetts. The Democratic Convention gathered with the same gaiety and blaring bands as its opponents, but considerably less united. In fact, it was divided on almost every major issue: the League, the Klan, Prohibition. The Party managed to adopt a plank favoring the League, but the one against the KKK was defeated by one vote.

Louis, Franklin, Al, and all the principal party men knew they had problems ahead; and Franklin knew as well as anyone that the choice of their Presidential candidate was the crux of the matter.

Franklin Delano Roosevelt had lost none of his old political gifts; in fact, his period of retirement with its opportunities for deep thought had improved them. The excitement in that huge, packed, hot, stuffy, tense hall increased when the audience saw him brought to the platform in his wheel chair and take his place with the other speakers. The whole grapevine knew that he was making a comeback this year, and he had hundreds of loyal admirers among them.

He looked out over the multitude and thought of the speech in his pocket and the effort and conferences that had gone into writing it. This was a tremendous moment for himself and Al. After the chairman had introduced him, he locked his leg braces straight, rose to his feet with assistance, accepted his crutches, and "walked" to the speakers' desk unaided. There was a subtle quiet pause of worry and admiration as he struggled across the platform—and he made it! When he reached the desk, he took a tight grip on the edge of it to balance himself. He surrendered his crutches, lifted his chin high, flashed a big smile at his cheering audience, and began to speak.

Peanut bags stopped rattling; lighted cigars went out unnoticed, mumbling conversations died to silence, even in the galleries. FDR told them of Al Smith's achievements as Governor of New York, of his ability to cut through red tape, of his integrity, his "power to strike at error and wrong-doing," his ability to make his adversaries quail. "He has a personality that carries to every hearer not only the sincerity but the righteousness of what he says. He is the 'Happy Warrior' of the political battlefield. . . ."

When he uttered the words "Happy Warrior" the convention burst forth in an ovation that drowned out the closing sentences of the speech. The joyful roar was for both Al Smith and Franklin Roosevelt. If only they could have nominated the nominator! If only he were well enough to run!

Thrilled, satisfied, happy, FDR found his way back to his wheelchair, and when the convention finally subsided he left the platform.

There was another star candidate in the field who had had the same kind of ovation: William Gibbs McAdoo of California. Capturing enough votes from McAdoo to nominate the Happy Warrior was going to be a tough job.

The whole convention proved to be a tough and tragic job, because when the delegates at last began to vote on the candidates, it became apparent that there was going to be a deadlock. But even those who knew political machinery well did not guess how long it would drag out. A convention had never come off its hinges so badly. On the first of July they were still in session, roll calling the fifteenth ballot—McAdoo 479, Smith 305½—and neither one could command a majority. Finally, on the eighth of July, with ballots nearing the hundred mark, FDR addressed the convention again. Al Smith would withdraw, he told them, if McAdoo would do the same. At first McAdoo refused, but after another day he and Smith both withdrew their names, and the convention nominated a dark horse, John W. Davis of West Virginia. It was a strong Republican year to begin with; now the Democratic Party had forfeited public respect, and it could consider the election as good as lost.

Two men prominent in that convention did not lose the respect of the public. One of them was Al Smith, who was re-elected as Governor of New York State in November. The other was FDR, the new FDR. The press went all out for him, and important political columnists even wrote him personal letters of admiration. The *Evening World* said:

"No matter whether Governor Smith wins or loses, Franklin D. Roosevelt stands out as the real hero of the Democratic Convention of 1924. Adversity has lifted him above the bickering, the religious bigotry, conflicting personal ambitions and petty sectional prejudices. It has made him the one leader commanding the respect and admiration of delegations from all sections of the land. . . ."

Chapter Nine

Warm Springs Interlude

AMONG THE MULTITUDE of people whom FDR met at the convention was a wealthy banker and civic leader named George Foster Peabody. Peabody spent most of his time in New York City, where he had his business, but he also had interests in Georgia. Shortly after the convention Franklin Roosevelt received a letter from Mr. Peabody telling him that he owned a place in Warm Springs, Meriwether County, about seventy-five miles south of Atlanta, Georgia. There was on the premises a natural pool of warm mineral water with a temperature of 88 degrees that he believed had curative powers. Near the spring there was an old resort hotel. He wanted FDR to try the spring, and to convince him enclosed a letter written by a local man named Louis Joseph who had lost the use of arms and legs from polio, but who could now walk with canes and no braces thanks to the pool.

That was enough to stimulate FDR's interest. He already knew the value of swimming and exercising his legs in water. In fact, he could by now stand up in water without his braces. The trouble with every place that he swam was that the water was too cold, and he could not remain in long enough. Now if he were to try this natural hot spring . . . where he could remain in the water for an hour or more without taking a chill . . . and if the minerals in it had curative powers. . . .

He did not even wait for Election Day. On October 3, 1924, he and Eleanor and Missy Le Hand—there always had to be at least one secretary around—arrived by train at the tiny station of the tiny village of Bullochville, Georgia. It had just been renamed Warm Springs for the sake of the Meriwether Inn. Through the train window they saw a group of eager people on the platform waiting to greet them. As Mrs. Roosevelt stepped out onto the platform at the end of the car one of them came forward. His name was Tom Loyless, he said, and they were soon to learn that he had been the courageous owner-editor of the *Enquirer-Sun* of Columbus, Georgia, and had been forced out of business because he had dared to speak out in his paper against the Klan.

Loyless had become interested in the old spa some five years ago and had leased it in the hope of making a go of it. He had not done very well, and two years before the arrival of the Roosevelts had persuaded George Foster Peabody to buy it.

With Loyless were Mrs. Loyless, Miss Georgia Wilkins and Miss Minnie Bulloch, both of local leading families, Louis Joseph on canes and no braces, and several others. By then FDR was out on the car platform, his heavily developed shoulders hunched up by his crutches. He flashed them his spellbinding smile and allowed himself to be carried down from the coach, placed in his wheel chair, and transported to Georgia Wilkins's car.

The sky was sunny, the air clear and warm and filled with the scent of pine. FDR hadn't realized that this part of Georgia was so hilly and had so much elevation. This ridge was Pine Mountain, his hosts told him, the southern tip of the Appalachian range.

When the car drew up in front of the Meriwether Inn, FDR threw back his head and laughed heartily. It was a big, old-fashioned, three-storied wooden structure, ringed with open porches at each floor, full of Victorian gingerbread trimming. Its roof was decorated with a square cupola that couldn't possibly have had any excuse for being there.

"A perfectly good down-at-the-heel resort!" he declared jovially.

He and Mrs. Roosevelt did not stay at the big hotel; they were soon settled in a nearby cottage belonging to people named Hart.

FDR was deeply eager to try the pool that had been built at the foot of the steep hill on which the inn stood. He wanted to know right away whether there was anything here that would help him. That was the next order of business.

From the moment that he got down on the edge of the pool from his wheel chair and eased himself into the water with his strong hands and arms, he felt a sense of relaxation as the warm water grew deep around him. It didn't taste of salts or other minerals as he had expected it to, but that was no real test. The most important thing to him at that point was that he could stay in the water for two hours if he wished, and he certainly did. He swam, he exercised, he played ball games with other swimmers, and he stood upright without his braces. When he was thoroughly tired, he dragged himself out and basked in the sun for another hour.

His old impatience took hold of him and showed plainly when he saw Louis Joseph walking around. Louis had recovered the use of his legs in this same pool, but FDR couldn't notice any improvement yet.

"It will take at least three weeks, Mr. Roosevelt," Louis and others cautioned him, "before you see any results at all."

But there was a national election coming up!

He and Eleanor decided that he must stay the three weeks and even longer and that she would return to New York to attend to political matters.

"Everyone is most kind and this afternoon Mr. Loyless has taken us for a motor trip through the surrounding country," FDR wrote to his mother. "Many peach orchards but also a good deal of neglect and poverty. The cottage is delightful and very comfortable and with Roy and Mary the cook bequeathed to us by the Harts who own the cottage we shall be most comfortable. The Loyless family are next door."

And so back to the pool, filled with waters that rushed up from a deep fissure in the earth at the rate of eight hundred gallons a minute. He spent every morning there, and in the afternoons he dictated letters to Missy, worked on his stamp collection for recreation, or toured the countryside with the Loylesses.

The pool was the focal point of his life during those first days at Warm Springs, and, due partly to his tremendous will to recover and his determination, he began to achieve improvement in his legs much sooner than anyone had predicted. In a few days he was able not only to stand up in the water without braces but actually to take a few steps.

One marvelous morning he called out to his companions, "I feel life! I feel life in my toes for the first time since my illness!" There was a noticeable tremor in his voice.

This was it! This was the answer! He must come here again and again. The next time he stood before a political audience there would be no crutches at all—maybe even no braces.

He concluded that he was his own best doctor, since the real doctors knew so little about his affliction and he knew best how he felt. With the help of a local physician he drew charts of the human muscles and learned the exact function of each, which muscles made the knee bend, which held it stiff, which were used in walking, standing, sitting.

He was ready now to believe the legend of the Creek Indians: that these warm waters had curative powers. Before the coming of the White Man, they brought their sick and their wounded warriors to the spring to cure and heal them. So much faith did they have in it that the place was respected as a sanctuary by all the local tribes and none was molested by his enemy while at the spring. How many "wounded" were there today who ought to be brought to this place to be healed?

"When I get back," he declared in another letter to his mother, "I am going to have a long talk with Mr. George Foster Peabody who is really the controlling interest in the property. I feel that a great 'cure' for infantile paralysis and kindred diseases could well be established here."

Upon returning to New York City, he talked to many more persons than Peabody about his discovery and progress. In January he began his new law partnership with Basil O'Connor, and on the first of April he was back in Warm Springs for six weeks. This time the impact of his dynamic leadership was felt in every direction.

Being a national political figure and having just made the Happy Warrior speech before his first appearance in

Warm Springs, the local newspapers had naturally covered his visit. One of them published an exaggerated article on him called, "Swimming Back to Health." It was syndicated in other papers and drew a lot of attention to him and to Warm Springs.

He was scarcely settled on his second visit, chatting with Tom Loyless and others about the possibility of developing the place into a health resort, when he heard that two paralytics had arrived by train and were down at the railway station. They had obviously come of their own accord, expecting miracles. FDR moved into the crisis and took over.

"Put them up at the hotel down in the village for the time being," he said, "while we fix up a place for them here."

There was an out-of-condition cottage on the ground which was hurriedly prepared and which FDR promptly named "The Wreck."

Others began to arrive as a result of the publicity until there were ten. FDR was delighted, but he had a few things to learn about hotels, especially vacation hotels. The vacationers at the Meriwether Inn stared coldly at the cripples when they appeared in the dining room, and when they found them swimming in the same pool they set up a howl of protest. They didn't want to "catch" polio. It did no good to explain to these people that there was no danger of catching anything.

At first FDR tried to ignore the controversy. He and

Louis Joseph got into the pool with the ten, encouraged them, cheered them, taught them to swim. He ducked Louis; Louis came after him and ducked him back. They tossed a big rubber ball around. There was a tall, skinny man from Pennsylvania, Fred Botts, and there were two fat lady patients whom FDR encouraged to get into the water and learn to stand. "Doc" Roosevelt helped them all.

But the clamor of the other guests grew too loud to be ignored, because the Meriwether Inn needed their patronage. So Franklin Roosevelt built at his own expense a second pool for his list of patients, and he had the ground level basement of the Meriwether cleared out and fixed up as a separate dining room.

Eleanor Roosevelt soon joined him at Warm Springs, bringing the almost nineteen-year-old Anna, Louis Howe, and Anna's police dog, Chief. It had done no good to warn Anna that Chief would suffer from ticks in the local woods. Anyway, the Roosevelt family never felt complete without at least one dog around. The boys were in school just then but they would see Warm Springs at the first opportunity.

Eleanor and Louis Howe soon joined the long conversations with FDR and others about FDR's dreams for the future of the place.

That summer he returned to Dr. McDonald in Marion, Massachusetts. Even though the water up there was too cold for that kind of therapy, Dr. McDonald was helping him in other ways. He had FDR walk round and round a square enclosure, holding on to the fence and dragging himself along without braces. Dr. McDonald taught him something else that was important to his personal safety: how to get himself around the room quickly by moving along the floor on his hands. If he were ever alone and the house caught fire, it would be just as well to know how to rescue himself.

By the end of the summer of 1925 FDR could actually walk several hundred feet on his crutches wearing one brace on the left leg. The right leg was beginning to come back.

He spent the winter in New York City working with Basil O'Connor to develop their new law firm, keeping in touch with political leaders, helping with The Woodrow Wilson Foundation, consulting with Tom Loyless and George Foster Peabody about Warm Springs. He was a man of many, many extra activities, but of them all two were now most important to him: the campaign for world peace through world government and the campaign to understand and conquer polio.

The plant at Warm Springs was losing money and couldn't go on that way much longer; Tom Loyless was not a very efficient manager. Roosevelt knew that Loyless was having serious trouble with his health, and he knew that Peabody would never have imagination enough to go along with the grandiose ideas for the place that FDR had in mind. There was only one possible solution: buy the place from Peabody and run it himself. There were gasps from his family when they realized what he had in mind!

"Franklin! That will take most of your personal fortune. It's never wise to put all your financial eggs in one basket!"

He just chuckled.

In February he bought the houseboat in Florida that he had been thinking of, the *Larooco*, and took a fishing cruise off the coast. While aboard he received word that Tom Loyless had died, and he immediately wrote a comforting note to Mrs. Loyless.

When he anchored at Key West, Charles S. Peabody who was George Peabody's brother, came aboard as his guest and so did William Hart, owner of the Hart Cottage at Warm Springs. FDR took them for a fishing cruise, and in the course of it he dropped into their minds the idea that he might want to buy the old Meriwether and all that went with it. When they returned to shore, he took them to the Key West Navy Yard, introduced them to all the naval officers that he had known since the war, took the whole crowd out to a delicious dinner, and, in fact, entertained them for four days. They left in the glow of a Roosevelt spell, and a week later he wrote to his mother:

"It looks as if I had bought Warm Springs. If so, I want you to take a great interest in it, for I feel you can help me with many suggestions and the place properly run will not only do a great deal of good but will prove financially successful."

Warm Springs was to be a rehabilitation center—as successful as he could possibly make it.

"Don't sign anything until I arrive. I'm taking the afternoon train," said a telegram from his law partner.

When Basil O'Connor arrived, the two men toured the premises, studied the sketches that Roosevelt had been drawing, and talked for long hours. Basil O'Connor was still doubtful of the financial wisdom of it all, but they decided to form a non-profit corporation and call it Georgia Warm Springs Foundation, and Basil O'Connor promised to draw up the papers as soon as he returned to New York.

FDR had already purchased the Meriwether and nearly twelve hundred acres of land on which stood the healing sanctuary of the Creek Indians, and before very long the new Foundation purchased the land from him, and he received a promissory note from the Foundation for the approximate $200,000 that he had already pledged to pay for the place in installments. But the Foundation would not have to pay him back until he died. He then took out a life insurance policy on himself for the same amount and made the Foundation his beneficiary. And when he did die, the insurance money cleared the debt. FDR was a clear-headed, shrewd planner; his wife, his mother, and O'Connor should all have remembered that fact.

As for running the place, he didn't intend to go off half cocked on that either. He was no doctor. As soon as he heard that the American Orthopedic Association was having its annual convention in Atlanta, Georgia, he persuaded them to send experts to investigate his place and make recommendations. They appointed a committee of three specialists. Next, he engaged the surgeon Dr. LeRoy W. Hubbard of New York, who had been treating polio cases for nearly ten years, Miss Helena T. Mahoney, who was a therapist and trained nurse, and a swimming teacher. They were to observe "Doc" Roosevelt's patients, work with them, and report all their findings to the medical profession.

He wished he could tear down the wretched buildings at once. They were tinder-dry wooden firetraps. Some day they would be replaced with safe, beautiful, modern structures.

Once he knew the place was his there was no controlling his enthusiasm and imagination. There must be smooth roadways and walks for crutches, ramps for wheel chairs. If he could not rebuild immediately, the dingy structures could at least have a new coat of paint. He drew more plans and sketches, jokingly calling himself an amateur engineer and landscape artist, and he began to invite all the wealthy people he knew to pay the place a visit.

Warm Springs was now for the patients—the pools, the dining room, the living quarters—and vacationers could find themselves another retreat. But it was still going to have all the charm of a vacation hotel, none of the barren grimness of a hospital.

By the end of May, 1926, the place was "open" and under the management of Egbert T. Curtis.

FDR returned to New York for some conferences with first officers and incorporators of this new non-profit corporation: Franklin D. Roosevelt, President; Basil O'Connor, Secretary and Treasurer; George Foster Peabody; Louis Howe; and others.

That done he was off in a whirl of his wheel chair to attend his daughter's wedding to Curtis Dall. Anna Eleanor, "Sis," was both his oldest child and his only daughter, and she had recently become old enough to be as much of a friend as a daughter, and so this was really a rather difficult separation. They had had their stormy moments. During the early part of his affliction she had been in the touchiest phase of her adolescence, and his impatience and gruffness had reduced her to tears many times. But that was all in the past. Now he must put on his cheerful countenance and see to it that her wedding would be something that she would always want to remember. He must be careful, though, not to steal the show from the bride and groom the way Cousin Teddy had stolen it from himself and Eleanor once.

The other big family event that summer was the graduation of his oldest son, James, from Groton: another tall, handsome Roosevelt. Were these tall men his "boys?"

In August he and Eleanor went back to Marion, Massachusetts, so that he could have another course of treatments with Dr. McDonald, and at the end of September he returned to Warm Springs for six weeks, taking his doubting, disapproving mother with him. He had begun building his own cottage, and he wanted her ideas about it and about everything else that he was doing.

Early in the year 1927 he went to Warm Springs once more, for the longest visit he had ever made there, from February 11 to May 12, and again from May 24 to June 11, this time to occupy his own cottage, to buy another twelve hundred acres, to refurnish the hotel with attractive appointments, to continue his own treatments, to make the thrilling discovery that between parallel bars on dry land he could stand for several minutes without braces, hands lifted in mid-air.

He was going to share this thrill with as many people as possible! Georgia Warm Springs Foundation must grow and expand and improve its facilities, and he was going to see that it did. Anyone who came to FDR to ask a favor, to seek advice, or to get on the good side of him for any reason whatsoever, could expect to spend part of the interview learning about Warm Springs.

Chapter Ten

Governor
of New York

MANY DID COME to FDR for an endless list of reasons, but most often they came for his political wisdom and talent. While he was creating the Foundation, he was working to re-create harmony in the Democratic Party. After the woefully undignified convention of 1924 there was a great deal to be done both within and without the party. He wrote to Democratic leaders all over the country, setting forth his ideas on what the party ought to stand for. It ought to be the great liberal party, champion of freedom and tolerance. It ought not to go either to the extreme left nor to the extreme right, but forward, and it probably needed a new Thomas Jefferson to lead it. "There is one common ground—Progressive Democracy—on which we can all agree," he told them.

He particularly wanted to see Al Smith nominated again, and he worked hard to bring it about. He even became Smith's floor manager for the convention.

He took Elliott, nearly eighteen, with him to the 1928 convention in Houston, Texas, as his aide and companion. Four years ago he had appeared before the convention on crutches. Since then he had achieved enough recovery of his back and abdominal muscles and sufficient balance in his braces, to be able to move about with a cane in one hand and his other hand leaning on his son's arm.

He was going to make the nominating speech again, to another sweltering, hurly-burly gathering, with one important difference: radio networks. The convention four years earlier had been broadcast by fourteen independent stations. This convention would be carried by two big networks, NBC and CBS, and it would be heard all over the United States. FDR was acutely aware that this new medium required a new technique in speaking. He composed his speech for the unseen audience, and when he came on the air he proved to his vast audience to be a golden voiced orator. His cultured family background and his processing through Groton and Harvard had given him beautiful pronunciation, and his strong, deep voice was made for broadcasting.

There was no deadlock this time, and Al Smith was quickly nominated. By June 30th FDR was back in Warm Springs, to have a good rest and prepare himself for the campaigning he intended to do for Al.

By now he had a whole court to assemble at Warm Springs, presiding over it like a happy king. The patients clamored for his company in games; the neighbors were eager to call and find out about the rumors they had heard that he might run for Governor of New York State; Missy Le Hand, living in her own cottage there, had his correspondence opened and sorted into neat stacks; Dr. Hubbard wanted to check his physical condition after the Texas convention; Miss Mahoney was waiting for him at the pool to resume his therapy; reporters from local newspapers had a question or two.

"What about the rumors that you are going to run for Governor of New York, Mr. Roosevelt?"

"Absolutely unfounded. I need to spend at least another couple of years on therapy before I can even think of running for election to anything."

He was more interested right now, he told everyone, in the new central heating system for the inn and the new indoor swimming pool that was being constructed. Among his many prominent friends who had visited Warm Springs so far were the Edsel Fords, and they had donated the money for an indoor pool so that the patients could have treatment all the year round.

He had another reason for not wanting to run just yet. He and Louis Howe and Eleanor rather agreed that this was not going to be a Democratic year. The country had been growing more and more prosperous under the Republican administration. There were plenty of jobs and plenty of money to spend. People would not want to risk changing that. If Al Smith defeated the Republican candidate, Mr. Herbert Hoover, in November, it would be by a very tight squeak.

Mrs. Roosevelt by now was almost as expert a politician as her husband, and she became head of the Bureau of Women's Activities for Mr. Smith's national compaign. FDR was convinced that she had more talent than he for getting a great many things done in a great many places at the same time. She was active in many women's organizations, worked for worthy causes, and kept up with her public speaking, all the while looking after her four sons —the youngest, John, had just entered Groton—and directing her four homes in Hyde Park, New York City, Campobello, and Warm Springs. And she was teaching school as well! She instructed girls in history and literature at the exclusive Todhunter School.

Franklin and Eleanor agreed that he would go back to Warm Springs in September and she would attend the Democratic State Convention in Rochester.

"You know how I feel about running for the governorship," he told her, and she nodded.

It was a wise reminder, because by this time FDR was second in importance in the party only to Al Smith himself, and in the eyes of many voters he was more so.

Scarcely had delegates begun to arrive in Rochester for the convention than the phone began to ring in Warm Springs. The party wanted FDR to run for Governor. He could poll more votes for them than anyone else. He said *no* again and again; he must continue his therapy. At last he stopped answering the phone and let Missy Le Hand do it. His right leg was really progressing; he wanted to get rid of that one brace!

But the party workers began to exert pressure in every direction. Even his daughter sent a wire urging him to run. He threatened her with a spanking, married woman though she was. Then he went off to Manchester, Georgia, to make a speech. While he was up on the stage of a crowded auditorium, waiting to be introduced, a note was handed to him that Mrs. Roosevelt was on the line. The call had been transferred.

After he had finished his speech he went to the phone, heard Eleanor's voice at the other end, but she only handed the phone over to Al Smith. The connection was so bad that he had the call transferred back to Warm Springs, and when he returned he picked up the call again.

"Frank!" pleaded Smith. "I will consider it a personal favor to me if you will run for Governor."

They must all be there, huddled around the phone to plead with him, because Herbert H. Lehman came on the wire to say, "Franklin, if you will run for Governor I'll run for Lieutenant-Governor and relieve you of a great part of the work."

Missy Le Hand must have seen a yielding in FDR's face, because she sat down and began to cry.

Smith came back on the wire.

"Frank," he asked. "If we go ahead and nominate you, would you refuse to run?"

"I don't know," FDR choked into the wire. "I don't know."

He handed the phone to Missy, but he could not look at her, because he knew that before the day was out he would be the Democratic candidate for Governor of the State of New York. There was some comfort in knowing that he would have a capable businessman like Mr. Lehman working with him.

While the convention cheered in Rochester, gloom settled down on Warm Springs. Nobody could even smile. Not only was FDR sacrificing his health, but his entire fortune was tied up in the Warm Springs project.

"I never knew a man to make greater sacrifice than you did in coming to the aid of your party," Mr. John J. Raskob, the General Motors executive wrote to him.

Mr. Raskob was Al Smith's campaign manager.

FDR let the gloom go on for a little while, but soon his voice could be heard booming across the swimming pools: "Well, if I've got to run for Governor, there's no use in all of us getting sick about it!" Laughter soon broke out again on all sides.

Early in October he returned to New York to start his campaign with headquarters at the Biltmore Hotel in New York City. Some of the people he engaged to work with him then remained loyal to him for the rest of his life. There was Miss Grace Tully as a secretary, because Missy Le Hand was ill and had to remain at Warm Springs. Another was the attorney Samuel I. Rosenman, who did a lot of work on FDR's speeches. Henry Morgenthau, Jr., soon joined the staff, and he, Rosenman, and Louis Howe made a terrific campaign team.

The opposition began to spread talk that FDR wouldn't be able to campaign because he was too crippled to run, but they were soon to eat their words. He *did* campaign all over the state with his usual thoroughness. As for "running" he declared with a burst of laughter that he was going to "walk in." Eleanor devoted her energies to the Al Smith campaign.

The election in November, 1928, was a pure tragedy for the Democratic Party, almost everywhere except New York State. The Republican ticket headed by Herbert Hoover swept in and carried forty of the forty-eight states. Even some states deep in the Democratic Southland went Republican. Some of that was due to anti-Catholic prejudice and some to the Republican trend.

In New York the results were close, so close that FDR wasn't sure of his election until the next morning. Tired but happy, FDR could dare to look back and count the number of years it had taken him to make this comeback —seven! He was only forty-six, still in his prime; he had plenty of time ahead of him and plenty of energy and faith with which to spend it.

The next order of business was another rest at Warm

Springs, then back to Hyde Park for an old-fashioned family reunion over the Christmas holidays, everyone around a gigantic Christmas tree in the living room, and everyone around the big table with its glittering crystal and silver, five young adults who had once been five small children, his white-haired mother glowing with pride and resigned to his political career, his devoted wife, all laughing and talking at the same time, catching up on news of one another.

But New Year's Day of 1929 was celebrated in a new way. That was the day of his inauguration as Governor of New York State. The old family Bible, printed in Dutch in 1686, its thick covers fastened together with brass catches, was brought from Hyde Park to Albany, and on it he took the oath of office.

He plunged wholeheartedly into the job, the way he always did, apparently forgetting that he had intended to let Mr. Lehman bear the brunt of it. The people he appointed to high posts in the state knew he expected them to do the same.

Even his opponents had to admit that he made good appointments, choosing capable people to fill difficult jobs. Miss Frances Perkins, who had been doing outstanding social work and was in the Department of Labor, he made chairman of the Industrial Board. Henry Morgenthau, Jr., became chairman of the Agricultural Advisory Commission, Samuel Rosenman the governor's counsel.

FDR was Governor of the Empire State for four years, and during his two terms he traveled everywhere and personally investigated its many problems. He consulted with farm experts at Cornell, talked with local government people, soon became a champion of a St. Lawrence Seaway, looked into labor and trade problems.

His personal aide and arm-to-lean-upon was Guernsey Cross. He could not expect one of his sons to be with him all of the time. They must complete their schooling and feel free to live their own lives.

As Governor he did not think of New York State as isolated and separate from the rest of the country. Farmers in New York often had the same problems as farmers in the West or the South; so did factory workers, and every kind of worker. He had always kept in touch with what went on all over the country, and now it was more vital than ever that he do so. It would not be possible to list all the prominent names with whom he corresponded while he was Governor, both in the United States and abroad. A few particularly stand out. There were Congressman Cordell Hull of Tennessee, Richard and Harry Byrd of Virginia, Will Rogers, Professor Felix Frankfurter at Harvard, Vice-Admiral Nomura in Tokyo, Prime Minister William Lyon Mackenzie King of Canada.

They shared their knowledge and experience with him generously because he was so gracious and outgoing himself. Here is what he wrote from Albany to a friend in San Francisco:

"This family is going through the usual tribulations. James is getting over pneumonia; Elliott is about to have an operation; Franklin, Jr. has a doubly broken nose and John has just had a cartilage taken out of his knee! Anna and her husband, Curtis Dall, are taking a short holiday in Europe and their baby is parked with us at the Executive Mansion. Eleanor is teaching school two and a half days a week in New York, and I am in one continuous glorious fight with the Republican legislative leaders. So you see that it is a somewhat hectic life."

From his correspondents he knew that times in 1929 were not really good. All through New England the economy was slowing down. Cotton growers in the South were having a local depression of their own. There were other danger signals out West. There was a great deal of bootlegging and gangster crime in the big cities as a result of Prohibition. Miss Perkins was sending him reports of rising unemployment in New York State, and this was his ever increasing concern. When the stock market finally crashed in October, 1929, the general public began to realize that the prosperity they had been enjoying was only inflation; by the time FDR came up for re-election at the end of 1930, the depression was under way and unemployment and discouragement were growing worse and worse all over the country.

But months before Election Day, Governor Roosevelt had faced the New York State unemployment problem squarely and had done something about it. One of his "glorious fights" with the Republican-dominated state legislature was to get them to pass unemployment insurance, but he could see that that was going to take a while. The idea was new; in fact, he was the first governor to come out for it. He did succeed in persuading them to pass a bill establishing the Temporary Emergency Relief Administration, known as the TERA, the first of its kind. The R. H. Macy & Co. executive Jesse Straus organized it, and a brilliant young social worker named Harry Hopkins was appointed as its chief executive.

Thus Harry Hopkins came into FDR's life, and like Louis Howe, remained completely devoted to him for the rest of his life. Hopkins had worked on the 1928 campaign, but not until his appointment to TERA did he and FDR really become acquainted. Hopkins had been born in Iowa and was about eight years younger than Roosevelt. Almost from the time that he finished college he had been drawn to some kind of social welfare work, and by 1930, when he was made chief administrator of TERA, Harry Hopkins was thoroughly familiar with poverty, slums, and unemployment. He knew exactly where help was most needed and how to administer it. In fact, other states quickly began to copy TERA to take care of their unemployed.

FDR was re-elected to the governorship in 1930 by a big majority, partly due to his record and partly due to the fact that the political tide was turning again. Of course, the party in power was being blamed for the depression, even though its causes went way back in history and even though similar depressions were happening in other countries of the world. When FDR attended a conference of all the state governors in Indiana the next summer, there was no doubt that he was the party's most popular prospect for the Presidency in 1932. He had won the confidence of the voters of New York State by showing that he had confidence in them. No other governor had chatted with them so freely and so often on the radio about their own problems. As Wilson had once ordered the ropes down to let the people in, he had ordered down stuffy traditions to let the people know what was going on. He told them of his bill for prison reform, to relieve the crowded conditions and poor food in prisons; this bill the legislature passed for him. He told them of his ideas for old age pensions, better working conditions, the building of new hospitals.

His courage in speaking out on issues sometimes upset party leaders. Prohibition was an excellent example of this. It was such a touchy subject that both parties were divided and afraid to take a stand on it. FDR was against it because he was against the bootlegging that gave gangsters so much money and power. He came right out for repeal of the law.

But when it came to the Presidency, a very awkward situation arose within the Democratic Party: Al Smith wanted the nomination again.

The friendship between the two top men of the party

had been fading slowly during the years of FDR's governorship, because, among other reasons, FDR asked the previous governor for very little advice, and he was gradually stealing the show from Smith on radio. Soon "Al" and "Frank" were battling one another in various state primaries around the country, trying to capture delegates to the Democratic National Convention. By the time the convention gathered in Chicago on June 27, 1932, they were almost neck and neck.

The Republican Convention had met smoothly and quietly just two weeks before in the same city and renominated President Herbert Hoover, as everyone expected they would, and there had been little excitement about it. But now. . . .

The Roosevelt family gathered in the living room of the Executive Mansion in Albany with party workers, secretaries, and friends. John and Elliott were home; Missy, Tommy, Grace Tully, Mr. and Mrs. Rosenman were there. FDR sat with a radio on one side of him and a direct telephone connection to Chicago on the other. Louis Howe and Jim Farley were on the spot at the convention, and so were James, Franklin, Jr., and Anna. The group waited through long, tense hours while the convention got into motion, elected a permanent chairman, and at last called for nominating speeches. The tensions were heightened by the squeals and static that even the best radios gave out in those days.

Nominating and seconding speeches went on all day

and into the night for the two principals and nine favorite sons. It was daylight in New York, nearly 4:30 in the morning in Chicago, before the roll call of the first ballot could begin. It stood: FDR 666¼ votes, Smith 201¾. FDR had a clear majority but he needed two-thirds. He smoked cigarette after cigarette in a long quill cigarette holder that Louis Howe had given him. Now the job for Farley and Howe was to persuade delegations to switch their votes from favorite sons to Roosevelt.

By the third roll call FDR's tally crept up to 683 and Smith's dropped back to 190¼. Good, good, but still not enough! The Texas delegation was still voting for John Nance Garner, and Texas had a big block of votes. If Farley can switch Texas, FDR thought fervently; if Farley can switch Texas. . . .

By that time the convention was wild and hysterical, because nobody wanted to give in and yet nobody wanted to see another deadlock that would disgrace them in the eyes of the voters. While the Texas delegates held a private caucus in Chicago, Eleanor Roosevelt went to her kitchen in Albany and prepared hot coffee and bacon and eggs for everyone. When the Texas delegates returned and their spokesman addressed the convention, Texas had declared for Roosevelt.

Wild cheering and commotion made the radio in Albany vibrate. Tired listeners forgot their fatigue and sat up. FDR grinned, and his strong fingers gripped the wheels of his chair.

William Gibbs McAdoo of California asked permission to address the convention. What did that mean? McAdoo was no Smith man. The deadlock between himself and Smith had forced him to give up his own ambitions for the Presidency.

"California came here to nominate a President of the United States," McAdoo began, and his voice could be heard ringing through the vast assembly hall. "She did not come to deadlock the convention or to engage in another devastating contest like that of 1924. California casts forty-four votes for Franklin D. Roosevelt."

McAdoo's hour of revenge!

The audience exploded. They went wild. This was the break-through!

With a happy shout FDR twirled the wheels of his chair and went scooting about the room. "Good old McAdoo! Good old McAdoo !"

His sons cheered, threw pieces of paper in the air. Missy ran to Eleanor Roosevelt and kissed her. Automobiles in the street outside began to honk their horns. Friends, neighbors, newspaper reporters came crowding in. Flash bulbs exploded.

"Have you finished going over my acceptance speech?" FDR asked Samuel Rosenman.

"Yes, Mr. Roosevelt."

Well, then, he was ready, and he was going to begin his campaign by breaking a tradition. Instead of waiting several weeks for a formal dinner at which to accept his nomination, he was going to board an airplane and appear at the convention while it was still in session.

Eleanor Roosevelt and John boarded the plane with him for a rather bumpy ride. Johnny became airsick, but FDR went right on putting finishing touches to his speech. James, Franklin, Jr., Anna, and the ecstatic Louis Howe met them at the airport, and all the way to the convention Howe and FDR fought over his speech in low tones, at the same time smiling and nodding from the windows of their limousine to the cheering throngs that lined the streets.

"Louie," FDR finally growled, "I'm the nominee!" and Louis left the speech alone from there on.

The hall was filled with the usual confusion, stale air, cigar smoke, and the exhausted delegates, ties loosened and limp, eyes red-rimmed from loss of sleep, were sticking it out to await his arrival. When they suddenly realized that he was standing before them on the platform, crutches gone, a cane in one hand, his left arm linked in James's right, they acted as though they had received an electric charge. FDR's heart swelled to bursting as he grasped the edge of the speakers' stand and began to speak in his golden-rich voice.

"I appreciate your willingness after these six arduous days to remain here, for I know well the sleepless hours which you and I have had. . . . The appearance before a National Convention of its nominee for President, to be formally notified of his selection, is unprecedented and unusual, but these are unprecedented and unusual times. . . ."

As he looked out over the sea of faces, he watched hope rising in them like a tidal wave.

"You can accept my pledge that I will leave no doubt or ambiguity on where I stand on any question of moment in this campaign."

The biggest question was the horrible depression and the thirteen million unemployed, and the fact that desperate, starving people were losing faith in their own system and turning radical. Carefully FDR outlined the remedies he wanted to put into effect. Farmers were hardest hit. "One-half of our population, over fifty million people, are dependent on agriculture; and, my friends, if those fifty million people have no money, no cash, to buy what is produced in the city, the city suffers to an equal or greater extent."

He wanted to save small home owners from losing their homes, because they couldn't meet payments on their mortgages. He wanted the tariffs lowered so that there could be more international trade. He wanted to create employment by reforesting the abandoned and eroded farmlands and by building much needed roads and parks.

"I pledge you, I pledge myself, to a new deal for the American people."

This was his mission. This was the service to which he belonged. To him had been granted the privilege of bringing the message of hope and courage to a people in the depths of despair and fear.

A man impelled by a great mission, he moved from the happy, weeping fatigue of the convention to the strenuous campaign for the Presidency. He traveled across the length and breadth of the land in a campaign train, and with him were James and James's lovely young wife, Betsy Cushing, his daughter Anna, and a host of news correspondents.

At home Eleanor Roosevelt with Miss Mary W. Dewson headed the Democratic women's campaign; Marvin H. McIntyre, the Washington news correspondent, became business manager for the campaign; and Jim Farley was chairman of the Democratic National Committee.

Wherever FDR went, he saw hope being reborn in the faces that looked up to him and listened to his adventurous ideas. This was like setting out in the *Mayflower* upon a vast ocean; no one knew what was ahead. There were bound to be storms; but it was challenging, thrilling, filled with unlimited possibilities.

As the opinion polls totaled up the results from week to week, he and his co-workers could see the tide of victory rising.

Often he chuckled to himself about the fears of those who had not wanted him to set out on such a long, difficult barn-storming—for fear he would *collapse!* And he knew that party men were irked because he was taking the political helm in his own hand and running his own campaign. Unheard of! But they were beginning to admit that he was as shrewd a politician as they had ever worked with.

The campaign issues were clear-cut in 1932. The conservatives and traditionalists were for Hoover; the liberals and adventurers were for Roosevelt. In old conservative regions like New England, FDR knew that there were many who could not bring themselves to vote for him no matter how much they liked him personally. His old Headmaster, Endicott Peabody, wrote to a friend just before Election Day: "Personally I am expecting to cast my vote for Hoover on the ground that he is in my judgment an abler man and that he has put into action policies which seem to me likely to relieve the economic tension in this country. I do not consider personal relations when I am casting my vote for a government official. It seems to me immoral to do so. . . ."

Franklin Delano Roosevelt wound up his campaign in his home state of New York, speaking to a huge, gay audience at Madison Square Garden and then making a summing-up broadcast from Poughkeepsie.

On Election Day the Roosevelt family went to the polls at Hyde Park and that evening they held a private dinner party for their close friends in their house on East Sixty-fifth Street in New York City. After dinner they all drove to Democratic headquarters at the Biltmore Hotel to listen to the returns.

The results proved to be a landslide. Roosevelt received a huge plurality of the popular vote and carried forty-two states. Long before the night was over, he knew.

This time he and his circle of friends and family were sober-faced, because they realized the gravity of the responsibility for all of them. The two United States Secret Service men who had joined them during dinner to protect the person of the new President would always be with them, because now their FDR, their Franklin, their Pa, belonged to the American people, and he must be carefully guarded at all times.

Mr. Roosevelt went to the Grand Ballroom for the photographers and into the microphone he said: "I want to say just a word. There are two people in the United States more than anybody else who are responsible for this great victory. One is my old friend and associate, Colonel Louis McHenry Howe, and the other is that splendid American, Jim Farley."

As soon as they could leave the headquarters, the Roosevelt family returned home.

The last person with FDR that night was his son James, who helped his father prepare for bed. Mr. Roosevelt could not dress or undress himself without assistance. James noticed without commenting how much of the paralysis his father had conquered. The muscles in the lower half of his body, his back and abdomen, were completely well and so were many in his thighs. It was the lower half of his limbs and his knees that had to be locked in braces when he walked or stood to speak.

As FDR lay back upon the pillows, James saw an expression of deep humility come into his face.

"You know, Jimmy," he said, "all my life I have been

afraid of only one thing—fire. Tonight I think I'm afraid of something else."

"Afraid of what, Pa?"

"I'm just afraid that I may not have the strength to do this job. After you leave me tonight, Jimmy," he went on, "I am going to pray. I am going to pray that God will help me, that He will give me the strength and the guidance to do this job and to do it right. I hope you will pray for me, too, Jimmy."

Unable to say anything, James withdrew, and Franklin Delano Roosevelt closed his eyes. He needed God, now, more than ever, because he must face his new task alone, completely alone.

Chapter Eleven

Attacking the Depression

BECAUSE HE NO LONGER belonged to himself, he must be more thoughtful than ever of his health; and so, between Election Day and Inauguration Day, which was not held until March in those times, he was able to take two vacations at Warm Springs. He was there for Thanksgiving, to preside gaily at a huge table, and to carve a gigantic turkey for patients and guests. Eleanor Roosevelt sat by his side and chuckled to see how he bloomed under all the adoration, especially from the ladies.

He had always been able to fill a room with excitement, and now that he was President of the United States the excitement around Warm Springs was beyond measuring. All sorts of national figures came there to consult him during his Thanksgiving visit and the visit toward the end of January. They came to discuss his new Cabinet appointments; ways and means of coping with the depression and unemployment; the banking crisis that was developing.

FDR had realized before this that his cottage was no longer adequate, and he had begun in 1931 to plan and build a larger dwelling. It is known today as the Little White House, and it was ready for him in 1932. It stands upon a slope of Pine Mountain behind the Foundation grounds, a simple colonial style house painted white. The walls inside are of plain pine wood, and none of the rooms is large. The living room and dining room are combined with a fieldstone fireplace at one end and a dining table and chairs at the other. His love of ships shows plainly in the porch on the back of the house. It is semicircular, like the fantail deck of a ship, and from its rail he could look out into the pine forests that he loved. Nearby he had a guest cottage built so that visitors could have complete privacy, and as soon as he had been elected, a host of Secret Service men had to have sentry boxes secreted among the trees all around the place.

The men assigned to protecting him had a time of it, because he loved to outfox them if he could. He had a specially designed Ford car with everything hand-controlled—clutch, brake, accelerator—so that he could drive himself around the countryside, and nothing tickled him more than to start off suddenly in his car and get out of sight before they knew where he was going. Then, when they finally found him again, he would roar with laughter.

In his heart he regretted all the changes that would have to be made in Warm Springs as a result of his election and the ways in which its quiet peacefulness would have to be disturbed. He regretted, too, that he would have to let others assume the responsibility for its direction. But by now Basil O'Connor had as much faith in the project as he, and although they could no longer be law partners, they could certainly work together on the conquest of polio.

FDR had dreamed of a beautiful great quadrangle of fireproof brick buildings at the Foundation, and of the day when the old Meriwether would be no more. That dream was beginning to come true. The Norman Wilson Infirmary had been completed two years before, built with funds raised by former patients and their friends and named for one of the patients. Georgia Hall was already in the planning stage, to be built by money raised by residents of the State of Georgia.

Promising himself that he would return to Warm Springs as often as possible, Franklin Delano Roosevelt journeyed north for his inauguration.

On the morning of the fourth of March, 1933, the Roosevelt family drove through the streets of the capital, waving to throngs of well-wishers, and attended service at St. John's Episcopal Church on Sixteenth Street not far from the White House.

Later in the day he stood where Woodrow Wilson had once stood, to take the oath of office, on his old family

Bible printed in Dutch. The weather was gray, chill, rainy, and the pressing crowds turned up to him faces filled with despair and discouragement. It was no secret to anyone that the United States was on the verge of economic collapse and chaos. Many in that crowd were hungry and had no idea when they would have another meal. The bottom had been reached, and still factories were shutting down, and banks were going under. There was no hope left except in the man who was about to speak, and the man who was about to speak knew it:

"I am certain that my fellow Americans expect that on my induction into the Presidency I will address them with a candor and a decision which the present situation of our Nation impels. This is preeminently the time to speak the truth, the whole truth, frankly and boldly. Nor need we shrink from honestly facing conditions in our country today. This great Nation will endure as it has endured, will revive and will prosper. So, first of all, let me assert my firm belief that the only thing we have to fear is fear itself . . ."

He watched the despair begin to leave their faces.

"This Nation asks for action, and action now. Our greatest primary task is to put people to work. This is no unsolvable problem if we face it wisely and courageously. . . . Our Constitution is so simple and practical that it is possible always to meet extraordinary needs by changes in emphasis and arrangement without loss of essential form. That is why our constitutional system has proved itself the most superbly enduring political mechanism the modern world has produced."

Faces began to glow, to smile.

"For the trust reposed in me I will return the courage and the devotion that befit the time. I can do no less. . . . In this dedication of a Nation we humbly ask the blessing of God. May He protect each and every one of us. May He guide me in the days to come."

He had said "action" and that was what he meant. He had already settled upon his cabinet. Cordell Hull of Tennessee was to be his Secretary of State. Harold Ickes was Secretary of the Interior. Henry Wallace was Secretary of Agriculture. Frances Perkins was Secretary of Labor. James A. Farley was Postmaster General.

All during his governorship he had gradually gathered around him a group of devoted specialists. Frances Perkins was one of these. Another was Raymond Moley, Professor at Columbia University, and Rexford G. Tugwell, an agricultural expert at the same university, and Adolf A. Berle, Jr., Professor of Corporation Law at Columbia. So were Samuel Rosenman, Henry Wallace, Basil O'Connor, Bernard Baruch, the financial expert. And there were Henry Morgenthau, Jr., and Dean Acheson, a Groton graduate.

They were not the usual men you would expect to find in government. The usual men had not been able to come up with a solution to America's dilemma. FDR, therefore, with his tremendous imagination and spirit of

adventure tried another kind. He tried scholars: econo-
mists, lawyers, agriculturists, men who understood the
theories of government. They became a conference around
him, and they were soon known as the "Brain Trust."

FDR, his Cabinet, and his Brain Trust, worked together
through long, hard hours, and after the Inauguration
Washington really hummed.

The opening weeks of FDR's administration are now
called by historians "The Hundred Days." During those
first hundred days he and his associates drew up and sub-
mitted to Congress fifteen new laws, all dealing with the
most urgent problems confronting the country. Since
there was a Democratic majority in both houses, FDR
received excellent cooperation.

The first and most startling of those laws was the Emergency Banking Act. Realizing that the panic that was
rising could cause havoc with the banks and wreck the
money system, he declared a bank holiday and closed all
the banks, two days after his inauguration. In another
three days he had a new law that made it possible to re-
open them on a more stable and sound basis.

By the end of March he had established the Civilian
Conservation Corps. This was to gather up all the desti-
tute young men wandering hopelessly around the country, riding the rails of freight trains, living as hobos,
drifting into crime, and put them to work refurbishing
the neglected parks and wasteland that had once been
forests. He put a forestry expert in charge of the program,

and soon more than a quarter of a million young men were going to camps, working in the open, jingling money in their pockets that they had earned themselves, sending money home to their families, and getting back their health and self-respect. Many of them had never been out of city slums in their lives before, and had no idea how much wide open space and fresh air there was in America. They eventually planted two hundred million trees that were needed to redeem land from erosion. They built irrigation dams, and they repaired national parks and restocked them with fish and game.

"Forced labor!" cried the critics, but FDR knew it was not. This was as great an emergency as a war, and these young men were enlisting.

Another famous law during the Hundred Days was the Federal Emergency Relief Act. This was to rush financial assistance to the states to aid the starving. As head of this task, FDR appointed Harry Hopkins, who had done the same job for him in New York State. It was a thankless job, and Hopkins became one of the most disliked men in America as a result, but he proved himself to be the best possible choice for a most disagreeable task.

Hopkins thought of the long, cold winter ahead, the fourth such in a row, and he knew from his years of experience in social welfare work that dole is the most humiliating way to help people. He created a Civil Works Administration, and by November he had four million unemployed people working all over the country. The CWA built roads, schools, playgrounds, sewers, and new parks. It employed teachers to give courses in adult education, and writers to write much-needed histories of every state in the union.

FDR had a special talent for making a person so enthusiastic and excited about his job that he was willing to work himself practically to death. He knew this, and he used his talent to the full to accomplish the kind of task that no President of the United States had ever before been faced with.

"We are priming the economic pump," he told the people.

AAA, or the Agricultural Adjustment Act, gave the President the authority to plan soil conservation and crops and farm produce on a national basis, and it stirred up a lot of discussion later on.

The project that stirred up the hottest argument was the Tennessee Valley Authority Act, or TVA. As usual, FDR went right ahead and ignored the brickbats of his opponents, because he had seen that poverty stricken valley on his automobile trips out of Warm Springs.

The Tennessee River begins near Knoxville in the Great Smokies, flows southwest into Alabama and then westward through the northern part of Alabama, and at last northward until it empties into the Ohio River. In the northwestern corner of Alabama, it churned and foamed through a shallow, rocky rapids called the Muscle Shoals, because of the masses of black-shelled mussels attached to the rocks.

Between Election Day and Inauguration Day FDR had written to Senator George Norris of Nebraska, "I have given a tentative promise to visit Muscle Shoals on my way to Warm Springs."

Norris was the liberal Republican from Nebraska who had been fighting for years to get a bill through Congress for a dam and flood control project at Muscle Shoals. President Coolidge had vetoed the first one, President Hoover the second.

FDR did visit the region as he had promised—more than once. He saw nothing but the direst poverty in wasted farmland from which trees had been cut until topsoil had been eroded away by spring floods that swelled the river and sent it spreading over the countryside. Then he sat down in earnest conference with Senator Norris and began to imagine through the entire valley a vast program of dams, cheap electric power for the region, reforestation, redeemed farmland, low-cost housing, new local industries, new crops. It would all mean employment, health, happiness. . . .

Senator Norris had not dreamed on so vast a scale, and he sat wide-eyed with hope for the poverty stricken region and all other such regions in the United States.

"That is the most wonderful and far-reaching humanitarian document that has ever come from the White House," he said.

But not everyone shared Senator Norris's opinion. There were some private power companies in the region who cried loudly that the government had no right to go into competition with private enterprise. In theory they were correct, but FDR was already hot under the collar about the too-high rates he was paying for his electric lights and power at Warm Springs served by similar power companies. They were charging what they pleased because there was no competition around, and they were forgetting their responsibility to the people they were serving.

The power companies involved engaged an attorney to represent them in the fight against TVA: the eloquent, dramatic, and brilliant Wendell Willkie. Willkie was President of Commonwealth and Southern Corporation, a public utility company which had some of its properties in the Tennessee Valley. Willkie, once a member of the Democratic Party, was a lot like FDR in many ways: a liberal, a golden tongued orator, a man who never did anything by halves. Roosevelt and Willkie were a match for each other, and Willkie carried the fight through the courts to the Supreme Court of the United States and made himself so famous and popular that he eventually ran against FDR for the Presidency. But FDR won the TVA battle and the project did redeem the valley.

Eight years later, Eleanor Roosevelt, who did her husband's traveling and observing for him, visited the region.

"A more prosperous area would have been hard to find," she said.

In June came another Banking Act creating the Federal Bank Deposit Insurance Corporation. This insured the safety of bank deposits of individuals up to $5,000.

Of the fifteen projects that FDR and Congress started during the first Hundred Days of his first term in office, the most popular for a while was NRA. NRA, or the National Recovery Administration (National Industrial Recovery Act), included practically everything that the other projects did not, and a few things that they did.

It was launched with a tremendous burst of publicity and parades and big posters and banners displaying its emblem—the Blue Eagle. The NRA asked industry to adopt a code calling for: shorter working hours, higher minimum wages, collective bargaining for workers, and an end of child labor in factories. It asked those working full time to give up a day or two a week so that some unemployed person could have a part-time job. All employers who adopted the NRA code were given a Blue Eagle sticker for their windows, and the buying public was asked to patronize those shops. In addition under NRA more public works programs were set up to create more jobs.

The American people took NRA to their hearts with great enthusiasm, and it added its effect to all the other projects that were setting the American economy climbing slowly but surely up out of the depths of the depression.

The pump-priming was working! The hopes FDR had raised during his campaign continued to mount.

Eleanor went on being his legs, traveling all over the country to check conditions that still needed correcting and the results he was achieving. She was never too dainty for any situation: squalid slums, sooty coal mines, farms, fishing wharfs.

"She ain't stuck up," said a Maine fisherman. "She ain't dressed up, and she ain't afeared ter talk."

Eleanor Roosevelt broke as many stuffy traditions while she was First Lady as her husband did as President. She made the White House a warm, informal, friendly place where grandchildren and dogs ran around freely and visitors felt at ease. The White House staff was startled by all the informality. FDR went right on being a jovial country squire, and Eleanor had no time to be a butterfly. If a staff member said to her, "Mrs. Roosevelt, that isn't *done* by a First Lady," she would reply, "It is now."

Living with them in the White House were their closest and most trusted associates. Malvina Thompson was still Mrs. Roosevelt's personal secretary, and Louis Howe was the President's personal secretary and confidant. Missy Le Hand and Grace Tully took care of most of his correspondence, with Miss Tully taking the greater part of the dictation and Missy doing the sorting and planning.

Stephen Early handled FDR's press relations, and Marvin McIntyre arranged his appointments.

President Roosevelt was at work every morning by ten, busy through the day with conferences and appointments, and those who expected to be working with an invalid discovered that they were exhausted long before the President. Late in the afternoon he buzzed for Grace Tully, who would come into the office with an armful of correspondence to be answered.

"Is that all we have to do?" he would ask hopefully.

"No, sir," was her reply. "This is all I could carry. There is more coming up."

After dinner he worked again, and he often took last-minute items to bed with him to read before he fell asleep.

The personal attendant who had the most to say about the President's activities was the newest in the picture. He was Vice-Admiral Ross T. McIntire, the President's physician. He was with his charge for the rest of FDR's life and checked his health almost every morning and every evening. He went wherever the President went in the United States and to foreign countries. Like everyone else he was amazed at FDR's good health; except for the lameness of his lower limbs, the President was in top notch condition.

Franklin Delano Roosevelt was really a relatively young man to be President of the United States. His first birthday in the White House was his fifty-second. He decided to devote it to the cause of crippled children, and on January 30, 1934, the first of the Birthday Balls was held in his honor to raise money for the Georgia Warm Springs Foundation. There were over six thousand such parties in cities and towns in the United States. At the chief party at the White House FDR spoke to the American people on the radio:

"It is only in recent years that we have come to realize the true significance of the problem of our crippled children. There are so many more of them than we had any idea of. In many sections there are thousands that are not only receiving no help but whose very existence has been unknown to the doctors and health services. . . . As all of you know, the work at Warm Springs has been close to my heart, because of the many hundreds of cases of infantile paralysis which have been treated there. It is a fact that infantile paralysis results in the crippling of more children and of grown-ups than any other cause. Warm Springs is only one of the many places where kindness and patience and skill are given to handicapped people. . . . Warm Springs, through the generous gifts which are being made to the Foundation tonight, will be able to increase its usefulness nationally, especially in the field of infantile paralysis. . . . No man has ever had a finer birthday remembrance from his friends and fellows than you have given me tonight. It is with a humble and thankful heart that I accept this tribute through me to the stricken ones of our great national family. I thank you but lack the words to tell you how deeply I appreciate what you have done and I bid you good night on what is to me the happiest birthday I ever have known."

That had not been his first radio talk since becoming President by any means. From the moment of taking office he followed the practice he had established as Governor of New York State—talking directly to the people about their own problems. Now he called his radio talks "Fireside Chats." The first, on the banking crisis, had been immediately after his inauguration, and in the simplest language he had explained that most difficult subject. In July he explained NRA. In January, 1934, came his appeal for crippled children; and before the year was out the Meriwether Inn, that old firetrap, had been torn down to make way for two new dormitory buildings at Warm Springs: Kress Hall and Builders Hall; and the staff was increased so that more patients could be treated.

Research scientists were beginning to make progress in developing a vaccine to prevent polio. They were certain by now that polio was caused by a virus, but they still had not *seen* it under the microscope, and they did not know how it traveled from one person to another. Dr. Maurice Brodie, working at New York University, developed a vaccine with killed virus. Dr. John Kolmer at Temple University in Philadelphia developed one containing the live virus. A hot controversy developed among research doctors over killed- versus live-virus vaccines, and the argument went on for years. But in 1934 and 1935, after many tests of both, the medical profession decided that neither vaccine was yet safe to use. There must be more research, much more.

Sitting in his wheel chair FDR understood the frustration a doctor felt when he could not help a child sick with polio because he did not know enough about it. He understood the frustration that doctors in laboratories felt who were unable to see the polio virus.

He had frustrations of his own. The depression was lifting, but not fast enough to suit him, and isolationist attitudes were still making it impossible to lead America into a world organization to maintain world peace. He must be as patient and enduring as the doctors in the laboratories, satisfied with a little progress here and there.

He had been in office only a few days when he proclaimed a special postage stamp to commemorate the 150th anniversary of George Washington's proclamation at Newburgh of peace between the colonies and England.

"The item in my collection [of stamps]," he wrote to Jim Farley, the Postmaster General, "which for me will always have the greatest personal historic interest is the Newburgh Commemorative Stamp."

And one of his most moving addresses during his first term as President was made at Arlington National Cemetery on an Armistice Day:

"We cannot and must not build walls around ourselves and hide our heads in the sand, we must go forward with all our strength to stress and strive for international peace.

. . . Jealousies between nations continue; armaments increase; national ambitions that disturb the world's peace are thrust forward." But he could give them one bit of assuring news: the new reciprocal trade agreement that had just been made between Canada and the United States. "I hope this good example will reach around the world some day. . . . If we as a Nation, by our good example, can contribute to the peaceful well-being of the fellowship of Nations, our course through the years will not have been in vain."

Chapter Twelve

Opposition

PRESIDENT ROOSEVELT had every reason to feel concerned for the peace of the world. Europe was becoming an armed camp all over again. Adolf Hitler, Chancellor of Germany since 1933, was growing powerful, ruthless, and military. Benito Mussolini had been steadily transforming the Italian monarchy into a dictatorship. On the other side of the world Japan had been at war with China since 1931. She had already conquered the region on the mainland called Manchuria and renamed it Manchukuo.

In 1933 FDR had sent a personal message to fifty-four governments urging them to agree to non-aggression and to curb their armaments programs. A Disarmament Conference of sixty nations at Geneva had come to nothing. FDR had sent a message to Congress in 1934 urging the United States participation in the World Court, but the Senate voted it down, in spite of all that he and Secretary Hull could do.

By the spring of 1935 Germany renounced the Treaty of Versailles and began to conscript young men into a new, big army, and by the fall of that year Italy had provoked an incident with Ethiopia and begun a military invasion. In another few months Ethiopia had been conquered and annexed.

The foreign picture was dark, but the picture at home was not yet as bright as it ought to be. The depression was not conquered by any means. There were still millions of unemployed.

At the beginning of 1935 President Roosevelt, his Cabinet, and specialists drew up a whole new work relief bill which Congress enacted. He hoped it would employ three and one-half million people. It had fifty agencies, and the best known of them were WPA, Works Progress Adminstration, with Harry Hopkins in charge; PWA, Public Works Administration, with Harold Ickes in charge; NYA, National Youth Administration; and REA, Rural Electrification Administration.

The National Youth Administration under the direction of Aubrey Williams, provided part-time employment to students in high schools and colleges so that they could continue their education; and it gave vocational training and employment to idle young people who were not in school. FDR had always insisted that federal aid programs be available to everyone regardless of race or creed. He appointed the dramatic and forceful Mary McLeod Bethune to take charge of the Negro division of NYA.

FDR was at his desk in the Little White House at Warm Springs on May 11, 1935, the day he signed the Executive Order No. 7037 establishing rural electrification, "a program of approved projects with respect to the generation, transmission, and distribution of electric energy in rural areas." This would not only create employment, but it would bring down the high cost of rural electricity, and it would give electricity to vast sections that still did not have any.

In the summer of the same year, FDR signed into law the Wagner Labor Relations Act and the Social Security Act.

President Roosevelt and Congress had been rushing ahead like galloping horses, growing excited and more excited as they saw the economy improve with all the projects and experiments they were launching. Suddenly a check rein pulled them up short. The United States Supreme Court declared NRA unconstitutional, and the vote had been unanimous. There had been a decision against one section of NRA a few weeks before, but this second decision brought the entire program to an end. Congress did not have the right to delegate so much authority to the President, declared the Supreme Court, and the federal government did not have the right to go as far as it had in regulating industry.

FDR was shocked. Now the biggest portion of his New

Deal program was ended and with it some of his finest intent: a floor under wages, a ceiling over working hours, and end of child labor in factories.

Looking at it another way, the Supreme Court had reminded him that the United States Government is a three-way plan: legislative, which is the Congress creating the laws; executive, which is the President administering and enforcing the laws; and judicial, which is the court system passing judgment on the wisdom of laws and the violations of them. Each department of the government is intended as a check on the other two, and the three balance each other out, so that no one department or person can ever take complete control of the government.

The United States had probably never had a stronger and more aggressive chief executive than FDR. He had been giving America more personal leadership than she had ever had from a President. Some felt that he was showing too much personal strength.

In his press conferences, newsmen found FDR as genial and charming as usual, full of humorous quips, ready to put off with a quick, brilliant remark any question he did not want to answer. When one of them asked him how he liked the Supreme Court's decision on NRA, he replied, "Oh, they are still living back in the horse and buggy days." It was true that a majority of them were seventy or more. Justice Owen J. Roberts, however, was only sixty.

And old age did not necessarily go with reactionary ideas. One of the most liberal men on the bench was Justice Louis Brandeis, and he was one of the oldest.

More test cases began to come before the Supreme Court, and the Court handed down more decisions unfavorable to the New Deal. It ruled against the much discussed AAA. But on the other hand, soon after the AAA decision, it upheld TVA, and brought Wendell Willkie's long fight to an end.

A side result of the NRA and AAA decisions began to be a more independent attitude on the part of Congress. It was definitely through being what the opposition called a "rubber-stamp Congress." From now on, FDR knew, the sledding would be tougher.

For FDR the 1936 campaign and election was the next order of business, and for this his closest and most trusted friend would no longer be at his side. Louis Howe, after a long illness, had very recently died, and no one would ever take his place.

Of course, Mr. Roosevelt was renominated by his party, and Jim Farley was in charge of his campaign as they went barnstorming to every corner of the nation. FDR made stirring speeches on the air.

"On this trip through the nation I have talked to farmers, I have talked to miners, I have talked to industrial workers; and in all that I have seen and heard one fact has been clear as crystal—that they are part and parcel of a rounded whole, and that none of them can succeed in his chosen occupation if those in the other occupations fail in their prosperity. . . . Do you have a deposit in the bank? It is safer today than it has ever been in our history. It is guaranteed. . . . Are you an investor? Your stocks and bonds are up to five- and six-year high levels. Are you a merchant? Your markets have the precious life-blood of purchasing power. Your customers on the farms have better incomes and smaller debts. Your customers in the cities have more jobs, surer jobs, better jobs. . . . Are you in industry? Industrial earnings are the highest in four, six, or even seven years. Bankruptcies are at a new low. . . ."

The Republican Party had nominated Governor Alfred M. Landon of Kansas to run against FDR, and the Republican campaign attacked all the weaknesses of the New Deal. It called the long list of agencies—CWA, CCC, TVA, NRA, AAA, PWA, WPA, NYA—"alphabet soup." These projects, the Republicans declared, were full of boondoggling. Too many Americans were developing the "gimmies" and expecting the government to support them. In many places these things were true. There were boondogglers, or fakers, holding jobs for the pay and only pretending to work; there were work projects that were started and never finished; some people were developing the "gimmies." There was a certain amount of waste and inefficiency.

But Landon could not deny the total result, and he could not compete with FDR's popularity with the voters.

When FDR's campaign train reached Chicago in the middle of October, thousands met him at the railway station, and nearly half a million tried to crowd into the stadium to hear his speech.

When he returned to New York, he gave his last big speech of the campaign in Madison Square Garden.

"For this final speech," he said to Samuel Rosenman, who was still working with him, "we take off the gloves."

Mr. Rosenman knew his chief meant it.

That night on the rostrum, FDR snapped his leg braces straight, rose, walked to the speakers' desk, and with head tilted up and chin protruding began to speak. He had never been in better form.

"For nearly four years you have had an Administration which instead of twirling its thumbs has rolled up its sleeves. We will keep our sleeves rolled up. . . . Of course we will continue to seek to improve working conditions for the workers of America—to reduce hours over-long, to increase wages that spell starvation, to end the labor of children, to wipe out sweat shops. Of course we will continue every effort to end monopoly in business, to support collective bargaining, to stop unfair competition, to abolish dishonorable trade practices. For all these we have only just begun to fight."

From Madison Square Garden he returned to Hyde Park to vote and to await the election returns with his family and neighbors. There were about fifty relatives and guests gathered, and Eleanor Roosevelt had arranged

a buffet supper. From the beginning of the earliest returns, FDR knew he was receiving an overwhelming vote
of confidence. Gradually the results mounted as he and
his companions sat in front of the radio, pads and pencils
in hand. His plurality was mounting so high he couldn't
believe it, and in the final tally he had won by a bigger
popular vote than any other candidate in the history of
thg United States. He had carried every state except
Maine and Vermont.

"Wow!" he declared, blowing a smoke ring into the
air.

"The blizzard of '36" was what the newsmen called it.

Even his old schoolmaster Peabody at Groton had voted
for him this time.

"In taking again the oath of office as President of the
United States," he said in his second inaugural address,
"I assume the solemn obligation of leading the American
people forward along the road over which they have
chosen to advance."

Confidence led to over-confidence, and very soon after
his second inaugural he began to reveal the secret resent-
ment that he had been harboring against the Supreme
Court for ruling against so many of his New Deal
measures.

Everyone has two sides to his personality, one attractive,
the other unattractive, and FDR was no exception. His
handicap had deepened and improved his attractive side;
it had also intensified his unattractive side, the side that

did not care to be crossed. To the frustration that he felt at being unable to walk freely and needing so much personal care was added the frustration of being unable to do all that he wished to cure unemployment, labor unrest, and the whole depression. The Supreme Court had just upheld the Social Security Act, but that was not enough, not nearly enough.

With great secrecy, consulting almost no one, he prepared a message for Congress. Then, on the morning of the same day that it was to go to Congress, he called his Cabinet and leaders of both houses together and read it to them. It called for revisions and improvements in the higher courts, but most important of all it was aimed at the Supreme Court. President Roosevelt proposed that all Supreme Court Justices be urged to retire within six months after becoming seventy and that the President have the power to appoint new justices, up to as many as six, in the place of those who ought to retire. If this became a law it meant that FDR would be able to appoint six new justices of his own choosing at once, because six of the present nine were at least seventy, and he could therefore increase the total number of judges to fifteen.

The men and women around the table sat in stunned silence. Was the President trying to make himself into a one-man government? Surely he must realize what a dangerous thing he was proposing. Why had he given them no time to go over this in careful conferences?

The daily newspapers were soon blazing with the announcement that the President was asking for power to reform the Supreme Court, and when reporters interviewed Herbert Hoover, he declared it a plan for "packing" the Court. Secretary of State Cordell Hull and Secretary of Labor Frances Perkins were both opposed to the measure but tried not to say anything to embarrass the President publicly. Their positions were too sensitive. Governor Herbert Lehman of New York spoke out against the bill.

A storm of controversy gradually arose everywhere. The Supreme Court was one of the most respected institutions in the land, a safeguard of the Constitution, and this proposal of the President's was frightening. Lawyers, historians, government experts spoke on the radio and wrote articles. Congressmen began to receive thousands of protesting letters from voters.

The President devoted a Fireside Chat to explaining his intentions to the public. The depression was by no means over, he said; one-third of the nation was still "ill-nourished, ill-clad, ill-housed." More national laws were needed to meet this problem. "There is nothing novel or radical about this idea . . . the laws of many states, the practice of the Civil Service, the regulations of the Army and Navy, and the rules of many of our universities and of almost every great private business enterprise, commonly fix the retirement age at seventy years or less."

The bill was referred to the Judiciary Committee of each house, and the Senate Judiciary Committee began public hearings in March. They listened for weeks to the testimony of lawyers, judges, Congressmen, labor leaders, business men. Many who had been loyal to FDR in the past parted company with him on this. Raymond Moley testified publicly against it. So did such Democratic Senators as Burton K. Wheeler of Montana and Carter Glass of Virginia. Chief Justice Hughes sent a letter of protest to the committee.

No national question was ever more thoroughly thought about and discussed as the hearings went on into the spring and summer. Compromise proposals were presented from time to time. The bill lost ground steadily.

In April the Supreme Court, which was going right on with its work, handed down a decision approving of the Wagner Labor Relations Act, which indicated that they were not trying to scuttle the New Deal after all. In July Justice Willis Van Devanter, one of the oldest members of the Supreme Court, reached his seventy-eighth birthday and announced his retirement. This gave the President a natural opportunity to appoint a new justice, and there were more opportunities ahead. In August Congress adjourned, and that was the end of the controversy.

After tempers had cooled many opponents of the bill began to feel that President Roosevelt had not been trying to destroy the democratic form of government after all, but that he had been unwise in creating an opportunity for some future President to do so.

Other critical news items took up the public interest.
There was a great deal of labor unrest and trouble in
the United States, big strikes in some places, and even
riots.

FDR had already begun to urge legislation to replace
some of the provisions of NRA, particularly a law to
establish minimum wages and maximum hours, but he
was not able to accomplish it before Congress adjourned.

He had no intention of giving up, and he took a trip
across the United States to see conditions for himself.
A business recession began in 1937, and when FDR returned to Washington he called a special session of Congress and outlined for them what he felt needed to be
done. One needed item was his wages-and-hours bill,
another was crop control so that farm prices would not
be forced down by the piling up of huge surpluses. The
number of people out of work had increased, and this
must be faced. And he wanted to see more supervision of
huge business trusts and combines.

President Roosevelt was still a man who could handle
many activities and interests at one time. He was watching the world situation carefully, and when he was called
upon to make a speech at the dedication of Chicago's
Outer Drive Bridge, he called for a quarantine of aggressor nations.

"The peace, the freedom and the security of ninety per

cent of the population of the world is being jeopardized by the remaining ten per cent who are threatening a breakdown of all international order and law. Surely the ninety per cent who want to live in peace under law and in accordance with moral standards that have received almost universal acceptance through the centuries, can and must find some way to make their will prevail. The situation is definitely of universal concern."

FDR had known for a long time how to feel the pulse of an audience as he spoke, and he could tell that Americans were beginning to realize that they could not really exist isolated from the rest of the world and what went on in it.

"It seems to be unfortunately true that the epidemic of world lawlessness is spreading," he went on. "War is a contagion, whether it be declared or undeclared. It can engulf states and peoples remote from the original scene of hostilities. We are determined to keep out of war, yet we cannot insure ourselves against the disastrous effects of war and the dangers of involvement . . . the will for peace on the part of peace-loving nations must express itself to the end that nations that may be tempted to violate their agreements and the rights of others will desist from such a course. There must be positive endeavors to preserve peace. America hates war. America hopes for peace. Therefore, America actively engages in the search for peace."

Many years had passed since Wilson's valiant appeal for a League of Nations.

There was a war that FDR was willing to declare and that was the all-out war on polio. In the autumn of 1937 he and Basil O'Connor began working together to create what is known today as The National Foundation, and FDR soon announced to the press that the organization would fight infantile paralysis in all three of its phases: before, during, and after. It would endeavor to finance responsible research agencies that were striving to understand the disease and find a way of preventing it; it would help hospitals give better care to those newly stricken with polio; and it would continue the rehabilitation treatments at Warm Springs and help other similar centers around the United States.

On January 3, 1938, the new National Foundation was incorporated with Basil O'Connor as President and Keith Morgan, who was already connected with Warm Springs, as Chairman of the Executive Committee. They hoped to be able to establish local chapters all over the country under the supervision of the national office in New York City.

FDR wanted to continue to dedicate his birthday to the polio fight, and the Foundation decided to make its appeal to small donors. During the depression years big donations had come in less and less often, and people were sending in coins, sometimes only a penny. The promotion task was assigned to a group of specialists in California. The best known member of that group was Eddie Cantor, friend of children everywhere. Eddie Cantor urged a radio appeal. He had recently raised a large sum of money for flood relief victims with only a thirty-second broadcast.

"I am sure," he said, "that all of the national radio programs originating in Hollywood would devote thirty seconds to this great cause. People could be told to send the money directly to the White House."

Heads nodded. So far so good, but there would have to be a campaign slogan, a lively idea or phrase to build the appeal upon. Eddie Cantor began to pace up and down. Suddenly he wheeled around with a big smile.

"We could call it THE MARCH OF DIMES!"

The planners adopted the idea at once, and FDR was delighted when the incident was related to him.

The first March of Dimes campaign was launched January 30, 1938.

The White House was accustomed to receiving about five thousand letters a day. On the first day after the appeal thirty thousand letters came, and mail trucks loaded with sacks of mail continued to arrive. Soon the joke began to circulate around the White House that nobody could find the official mail.

After all the criticisms he had been living through this past year, President Roosevelt found the response very heartwarming and comforting indeed.

That same summer the first research grants went out to universities, hospitals, and other professional groups. The war against polio was on!

The contagion of real war was still spreading around the world. Aggressor nations were growing bolder and bolder. Just the previous December Japanese bombers had sunk the United States gunboat, *Panay*. In March, 1938, Germany invaded and annexed Austria. By fall Hitler had created a crisis with Czechoslovakia and was soon demanding a whole northern section of the country known as the Sudeten region. Prime Minister Neville Chamberlain of Great Britain went in person to confer with Hitler at Berchtesgaden. Later there was a conference in the city of Munich of Hitler, Chamberlain, Mussolini, Édouard Daladier of France; and they advised Czechoslovakia to give up the Sudeten region for the sake of world peace.

When FDR gave his annual message to Congress in January, 1939, it was mostly about war. He wanted Congress and the American people to realize that the "new philosophies of force were to encompass the other continents and invade our own." It was true that Congress had passed a Neutrality Act prohibiting the shipment of arms and lending of money to warring nations. But he wanted them to begin thinking seriously of the state of their own defenses. This was going to mean higher taxes.

Hitler's word proved to be worth nothing as far as the Munich Pact was concerned. In spite of his assurances that he wanted no further territory he soon seized the rest of Czechoslovakia. The whole world waited in tense fear. Apparently Poland was going to be next. Austria had not resisted; Czechoslovakia had not resisted; Poland did. That was Hitler's excuse to attack, and his planes began to bomb the city of Warsaw. Great Britain and France, who had agreed that they would assist Poland if she were attacked, both declared war on Germany. World War II had begun.

On the third of September, 1939, President Franklin Delano Roosevelt went on the air:

"Until four-thirty this morning I had hoped against hope that some miracle would prevent a devastating war in Europe and bring to an end the invasion of Poland by Germany." He cautioned Americans to be calm and objective, to "discriminate most carefully between news and rumor."

"Let no man or woman thoughtlessly or falsely talk of America sending its armies to European fields. At this moment there is being prepared a proclamation of American neutrality. . . . I have said not once, but many times, that I have seen war and that I hate war. I say that again and again. I hope the United States will keep out of this war. I believe that it will. And I give you assurance and reassurance that every effort of your Government will be directed toward that end. As long as it remains within my power to prevent, there will be no blackout of peace in the United States."

He had begun to relive Woodrow Wilson's anguish.

Chapter Thirteen

Global War

TRAGIC EVENTS rushed along in Europe during the next year. Before Hitler attacked Poland he had signed a non-aggression pact with Russia so that he would be safe on his eastern side. France and England were mobilizing and arming as fast as they could, but Hitler's military might seemed invincible. His armies spread out and occupied Norway and Denmark, Belgium and the Netherlands. The French had constructed a long line of defense called the Maginot Line from Switzerland to Belgium, but the German forces rushed around it and into northern France like a river in spring flood. Nearly 400,000 troops, mostly British, were trapped and surrounded along the beaches at Dunkirk, and for a whole week, while enemy shells burst all around them and the British Air Force gave what protection it could, every kind of boat, rowboat, sailboat, fishing vessel, anything that would float, was rushed to evacuate them across the English Channel. By the middle of June, France surrendered, and the Nazi forces swept through Paris and across France. Italy entered the war as a member of the Axis and the combat spread to North Africa. The "Battle of Britain" began, and planes bombed English cities almost every night. Japan joined the Axis.

FDR began to gather around him the most capable advisers he could find. Many top business executives eventually worked for a dollar a year. The President appointed Henry L. Stimson, who had held the post before World War I, as his Secretary of War. He made Frank Knox, once a foe of the New Deal, Secretary of the Navy, Henry Morgenthau, Jr., had been Secretary of the Treasury for several years, and Cordell Hull was Mr. Roosevelt's Secretary of State during almost his entire time in office.

Around the same time Winston Churchill replaced Neville Chamberlain as Prime Minister of the British Commonwealth.

In the midst of all the stress and strain of world affairs, 1940 was a Presidential Year, and meeting so soon after Dunkirk and the fall of France both parties were destined to have exciting conventions.

The Republicans gathered in Philadelphia the third week of June, and the top four contenders for the nomination were Thomas E. Dewey of New York, Senator Robert A. Taft of Ohio, Wendell L. Willkie of Indiana, and Senator Arthur H. Vandenberg of Michigan. On the first ballot of pledged votes they were in that order with Dewey leading with 360 votes and Willkie third with 105.

Willkie's popularity as a leader of the opposition to the New Deal had been snowballing ever since his TVA fight. He had been speaking to large gatherings and on the air. When he debated another speaker on a national issue, he usually pulverized his opponent. He was unquestionably an able, brilliant man with a worldwide point of view and plenty of courage, and as his popularity continued to snowball at the convention, excitement snowballed with it. Each ballot increased his score until he was top of the list. On the fifth ballot he had 429, and on the sixth he had the nomination.

For many weeks preceding the Democratic National Convention, which was held in Chicago in July, there was a great deal of talk circulating as to whether FDR would run for a third term. Such a thing had never been done before. George Washington himself had established the precedent by refusing to run for a third term. But Willkie was going to be hard to beat, and FDR was the strongest candidate the party had. FDR was rapidly becoming a world leader with influence among other world leaders at a time when many realized that the United States was teetering on the brink of World War II.

Mr. Roosevelt himself kept silent on the subject, because the idea of at last being able to return to Hyde Park and the Hudson River Valley did appeal to him. But Mrs. Roosevelt knew that he would not refuse to run if nominated. FDR thought it over carefully. What other candidate did the Democratic Party have who could bring all the national and international experience to the task that would be needed in the next few years? The only man in his opinion was Secretary of State Cordell Hull. But when FDR approached him, Hull would have no part of it. He would not even run for Vice-President. He could be of more service where he was, he declared, especially if he stayed out of party contests. This could mean but one thing. The Democratic National Convention, after receiving a message from the President that he had no desire to run again, placed his name immediately in nomination. Other men were nominated, among them Jim Farley and Cordell Hull, but on the first ballot FDR received 946½ votes, and Jim Farley immediately moved that it be made unanimous. FDR was the candidate again by acclamation.

The 1940 Presidential campaign was one of the most colorful and fascinating that America had ever seen. On both sides thousands worked in it who had never taken part in politics before, especially young people. The times were grave; the issues were grave. The decision that voters had to make was never more serious. Yet, both candidates were liberal, international, and in favor of similar things. It was really a battle between two remarkable personalities. Nearly fifty million people went to the polls on Election Day, the largest total vote that had ever occurred in a national election.

FDR chalked up another victory. He received five million more popular votes than Willkie, and he carried all but ten states.

While he sat with Mrs. Roosevelt at Hyde Park listening to the result, he realized that the eight years he had just completed had taken a great toll of his energies. Ordinarily eight years in the Presidency would be thought enough of a contribution for a man to make, especially considering the extraordinary problems he had had to face. But there were greater problems ahead, and the American people had asked him to serve for four more years. The war clouds were growing blacker.

Blacker than any war cloud could ever be, a new member joined the Roosevelt family circle shortly after Election Day, and in spite of his blackness he brought light and happiness into the household. His name was Murray the Outlaw of Fala Hill, and he was an eight-month-old Scottie dog, a gift from FDR's distant cousin, Miss Margaret Suckley. FDR shortened the dog's name to Fala, and no dog ever meant as much to him. From then on Fala was seen in the news pictures almost as often as the President, because they were usually together.

Fala liked life at the White House. Each morning after his walk he bounded into the President's bedroom and up on the bed, looking for the dog biscuit on the President's breakfast tray. And each evening, no matter how trying the day had been, the President spent some time with Fala before he retired. Fala inspected defense plants and attended history making conferences; he rode in the official car and gave press interviews.

In December Fala accompanied the President to Warm Springs for a much needed rest.

Thanks to FDR's generous friends and the March of Dimes, the plant at Warm Springs was still growing and improving. A chapel had been built in 1937, chiefly with funds donated by Miss Georgia Wilkins, where services were held for Catholic, Protestant, and Jewish patients. It had only a few pews and plenty of space for wheel chairs and stretchers. The next year the Brace Shop had been opened, and there every kind of appliance to suit the individual patient was being designed and experimented with. FDR's own leg braces had once weighed forty pounds, and now they weighed only twenty, because a lighter type of brace had been developed there. Just the previous year the School and Library had been built, a gift of Mrs. S. Pinkney Tuck, where children and young people could continue their regular schooling while they were at Warm Springs for treatment. And the Medical Building was completed where orthopedic surgeons could perform operations to improve the movements of the handicapped.

The electron microscope had recently been perfected, making far greater magnification possible, and some types of virus had already been seen and photographed. Perhaps this would mean that eventually scientists would *see* the polio virus, thought to be one of the smallest of the viruses.

It was comforting to know that, while men in so many places were plotting and planning to destroy human life and happiness, life-saving research was still going on.

Rested, President Roosevelt returned to Washington, to give before a joint session of Congress his famous speech on the "Four Freedoms." The four freedoms, he told Congress, are freedom of speech and expression, freedom of worship, freedom from want, and freedom from fear. He made it entirely clear that all of those freedoms had never been in more danger of being wiped out. He knew how grave his words were, and so did everyone who was listening. His own four sons were all destined for military service. James, in his early thirties, had been in the Marine Corps Reserve for nearly four years; Elliott volunteered for the Army Air Corps; Franklin, Jr., was in the Naval Reserve; and John, the youngest, was soon to be commissioned as an Ensign.

About a month after his "Four Freedoms" speech Congress passed a Lend-Lease Bill allowing the United States to send money and materials to the Allies.

Still Hitler expanded. In June he forgot his pact with Russia and launched a military offensive against her.

President Roosevelt and Prime Minister Churchill wanted to meet. Each had said so. Each was hard pressed by the responsibilities of office, but in August, 1941, with the utmost secrecy, they finally were able to consult for three days. Prime Minister Churchill came on board the H. M. S. *Prince of Wales* and the President aboard the U. S. S. *Augusta* to Argentia Harbor, New-foundland, on Placentia Bay, protected by ships, air-planes, troops ashore, and foggy weather.

Among the party that accompanied the President were Undersecretary of State Sumner Welles, carrying the draft of a precious document, several generals including Chief-of-Staff General George C. Marshall, several admirals, and Harry Hopkins, who had been in England. Since Elliott and Franklin were on duty in the area, the President was able to have two of his sons with him.

At the first formal dinner of the sessions everyone found Churchill to be a spellbinder when he discoursed on and on, and the President encouraged him with an occasional question. Elliott later wrote a careful account of the meetings. "He slewed his cigar around from cheek to cheek and always at a jaunty angle, he hunched his shoulders forward like a bull, his hands slashed the air expressively, his eyes flashed."

Churchill had come, it was soon apparent in subsequent sessions, to persuade the United States to enter the war. President Roosevelt had come to plan for world peace after the war. Slowly and carefully President Roosevelt assumed a dominant role.

"I am firmly of the belief that if we are to arrive at a stable peace it must involve the development of backward countries. Backward peoples. How can this be done? It can't be done, obviously, by eighteenth-century methods," said FDR.

He was pointing directly at conditions in some of the colonies of the British Dominions, and Mr. Churchill knew it.

Both men were eloquent, strong-willed, but in the final analysis it was Mr. Roosevelt's point of view that won out.

"Peace cannot include any continued despotism," he insisted. "The structure of the peace demands and will get equality of peoples."

While they did not agree on everything, the two men admired and respected each other, and long before the conference was over they were calling each other by their first names. The most important reason for meeting was the draft that Mr. Welles had brought and that he had prepared for this occasion, the draft of the document known today as the Atlantic Charter. After both men were safely back in their capitals, the text was released along with news reports of their conferences.

The Atlantic Charter stated that the two countries sought no new territories for themselves; that they respected "the right of all peoples to choose the form of government under which they will live"; that after the war they would strive to help other countries, large and small, achieve prosperity, and improve their economic standards; and that they "hope to see established a peace which will afford to all nations the means of dwelling in safety within their own boundaries, and which will afford assurance that all the men in all the lands may live out their lives in freedom from fear and want."

As he had prayed for strength on first being elected to the Presidency, FDR still prayed for the strength and the wisdom to make these hopes come true. He felt more alone than ever in his high office and often wished that he could have had Louis Howe still with him. Missy Le Hand had been taken seriously ill last summer and would never be able to work with him again. His sons were on duty. And shortly after his meeting with Churchill, Sara Delano Roosevelt died. She was eighty-six, but she had remained vigorous and active almost to the end, living in New York City and making frequent visits to the White House.

The President's physician was finding him less and less willing to spare himself, because his responsibilities were growing more and more gigantic. The war in Europe was now three years old; German submarines were growing as bold as they had in the previous war and much more efficient. Lend-Lease was stepped up, and United States merchant ships were armed. At the same time FDR and Secretary Hull were holding conferences with the Japanese Ambassador and other diplomats from Japan to forestall war in the Pacific, and it appeared that Japan was as much in earnest as they about it.

They had been misled.

Early Sunday afternoon, December 7, 1941, President Roosevelt received a telephone call from Secretary Knox telling him that Japanese planes had attacked the United States fleet in Pearl Harbor, Hawaii.

Shocked, angry, sickened by the treachery, FDR sent immediately for those closest and most important to him: Eleanor Roosevelt, who was receiving guests in another part of the White House; James, who happened to be near Washington; Harry Hopkins; Secretary Hull; Secretary Knox; Secretary Stimson; General Marshall; Grace Tully. Everyone's face looked older, ghastly white, as they listened to one news bulletin after the other. Every battleship of the Pacific fleet disabled, five of them sunk; cruisers, destroyers, submarines damaged; more than two thousand Navy and Marine Corps men lost.

When James Roosevelt arrived, FDR looked up at him and said, "Hello, Jimmy. It's happened."

The President ordered a Cabinet meeting for that evening and by five o'clock he was ready to dictate his message to Congress.

"Sit down, Grace. I'm going before Congress tomorrow. I'd like to dictate my message. It will be short."

She obeyed.

"Yesterday comma December 7 comma 1941 dash a day which will live in infamy dash the United States of America was suddenly and deliberately attacked by naval and air forces of the Empire of Japan period paragraph."

The message was short and to the point, and when he delivered it to Congress the next day it took only six minutes.

"Hostilities exist. There is no blinking at the fact that our people, our territory and our interests are in grave danger . . . I ask that the Congress declare that since the unprovoked and dastardly attack by Japan on Sunday, December 7th, a state of war has existed between the United States and the Japanese Empire."

During the hours that he spent writing the message, the Japanese had attacked Malaya, Hong Kong, Guam, the Philippines, Wake, and Midway.

The declaration of war by Congress that followed meant complete mobilization of the nation—agriculture, industry, men and women—suspension of all sorts of personal freedoms and liberties—everything that a free democratic society does not stand for, with the President required to assume the role of Commander-in-Chief. If these freedoms and privileges were returned to the people when the war was over, it would be due in large measure to the integrity of the men and women in office—in power, really—during the war.

The year 1942 was the darkest in America's history, and the darkest of World War II. But during it and the years that followed Franklin Delano Roosevelt rose to his greatest stature as President of the United States and as one of the three top leaders of the world. He, Prime Minister Churchill, and Joseph Stalin of Russia eventually became known as "The Big Three."

FDR never lost sight of his long-range goal. On the first day of that darkest year the representatives of twenty-six nations, in Washington, D.C., signed the United Nations Declaration, approving the Atlantic Charter and agreeing not to make any separate peace with the Axis. Churchill had come to Washington in person for that occasion, and he returned again in June for further combined planning. By then the Japanese had conquered Wake, Singapore, New Guinea, the Philippines, the Aleutians, and Midway; and the Axis armies were pushing the British Eighth Army back in North Africa.

Yet, in that same darkest of years, an incident occurred that very few people knew about and that the newspapers had no space to report. A promising young intern at Mount Sinai Hospital in New York City received a fellowship from The National Foundation to do research at the University of Michigan in contagious diseases and vaccines. His name was Dr. Jonas E. Salk.

In the fall Eleanor Roosevelt went to England on her first war trip. There she exchanged ideas with the British government on Civilian Defense Work, visited Red Cross Clubs and the wounded in hospitals. All during the war she had a most strenuous schedule to which her travels were added. She also wrote a newspaper column, and her earnings from that went half to the Red Cross and half to the American Friends Service Committee. After her next war trip—to the Pacific theater—where she saw so many wounded young men and so many young people deranged from their experiences, she came home with one question in her mind, "Why does this have to happen?"

Driven by the same question, President Roosevelt himself went to North Africa in January of 1943. There for ten days at Casablanca he met with Churchill, General Charles de Gaulle of France, Generals Dwight Eisenhower and Marshall, Admiral Ernest King, and high ranking British officers to plan further strategy.

"We and all the United Nations want a decent peace and a durable peace," he had said to Congress just before setting out for North Africa, and at Casablanca he spoke of the postwar organization that he had in mind.

By this time there was a deep personal understanding between Churchill and Roosevelt, but he found General de Gaulle to be quite different. The French leader was temperamental and aloof.

All four of FDR's sons were in combat by now, and it was particularly comforting to him to be able to see Elliott and Franklin while he was at Casablanca. Elliott was a reconnaissance pilot; Franklin was aboard the destroyer *Mayrant* in the Mediterranean. John was on an aircraft carrier "somewhere," and James was with Carlson's Raiders in the Pacific. Anna's husband was in the army.

He insisted on seeing as much as he could while he was in North Africa. In spite of the fierce sun and the exhausting sessions on strategy, he went out in a jeep to view the troops, and he flew over devastated battle areas.

The next big conference of Allied leaders was in December of 1943, at Teheran, the capital of neutral Iran, or Persia, and at that meeting he learned to know yet another personality: Joseph Stalin. He found Stalin to be rather short and stocky in appearance but with an iron will, somber, and suspicious, not at all eager to involve his country in any world organization after the war.

Combining such different personalities and nations for their mutual benefit was difficult. Much of the burden for their unity fell upon FDR, and he realized that after the war, when they were beginning to feel safe again, combining them would be even more difficult.

The tide had already turned in North Africa, on the Russian front, and in Burma; and the Allies had almost completed their invasion of Italy when the invasion of the Continent along the beaches of Normandy was announced: "D" Day, June 6, 1944—the strategy that had been worked out at Teheran.

By the middle of July, FDR was en route to Hawaii to consult with the two top commanders there: General Douglas MacArthur and Admiral Chester Nimitz. While he was in the Pacific theater, he made a personal tour of the hospitals to visit the wounded men, and many of them could not believe that it was really he. He'd been stricken once himself, and so he knew how to talk to stricken men. He understood the discouragement a man feels when he realizes he has a sudden and new handicap to cope with. FDR came through the wards booming with laughter, cracking jokes, and his heart warmed to see the men perk up and laugh back.

On his return to the United States he was officially advised that the Democratic National Convention had nominated him to run for a fourth term, and they expected a big result for him at the polls. Automatic elections, so necessary to a democratic society, were one of the privileges that had not been suspended during the war.

Franklin Delano Roosevelt was the dominating personality of the western world. It was his diplomacy that won cooperation from De Gaulle, he who struck a balance between Churchill and Stalin, he who had the vision and the dedication to see the dangers of the peace ahead and how those dangers must be met. While he was in Hawaii a preliminary United Nations meeting of forty-four countries was going on at Bretton Woods, New Hampshire, to work out the banking and money problems of the postwar world. At Bretton Woods the plans were completed for an International Bank, a very necessary first step for setting world trade into motion once more. FDR had made that step possible.

The next step was a meeting the following month at Dumbarton Oaks, an estate in Washington, D.C., of diplomats from China, Russia, Great Britain, and the United States to draft a preliminary Charter of the United Nations. Not all of their differences were yet ironed out, but President Roosevelt estimated that they were in ninety per cent agreement.

After Dumbarton Oaks he hurried to Quebec for another meeting with Winston Churchill.

In November he received his overwhelming vote of confidence from the American people and shortly after Election Day went to Warm Springs for a rest. He was deeply tired, many pounds underweight, although a thorough physical examination by Admiral McIntire and five other consulting physicians found him to be in excellent health. He had seen very little of Warm Springs after America's entry into the war. In 1942 he had not been there at all, and only once in 1943 and 1944.

But FDR's immediate family did not share his doctors' optimism about his health. When James came home to be at his side for the inauguration, he was shocked and alarmed by his father's appearance. Laying a hand on his oldest son's arm, FDR admitted that he would have a difficult time getting through the ceremonies. Yet, when father and son sat talking, the President's only concern was for his next "Big Three" conference. He wanted to be there to help fashion a just and lasting peace.

"We can and we will achieve such a peace," he said in his fourth Inaugural Address. "We have learned that we cannot live alone, at peace; that our own well-being is dependent on the well-being of other nations—far away. We have learned that we must live as men, not as ostriches, nor as dogs in the manger. We have learned to be citizens of the world, members of the human community. We have learned the simple truth."

The "Big Three" Conference was at Yalta, on the Crimean coast of the Black Sea in southern Russia, February, 1945. There Roosevelt, Churchill, and Stalin agreed on many territorial and truce terms, ironed out a few more differences for the United Nations, and agreed to send representatives to a conference in San Francisco in April to found a United Nations Organization.

"Dearest Babs," FDR wrote to Mrs. Roosevelt. "We have wound up the conference—successfully I think and this is just a line to tell you that we are off for the Suez Canal and then home but I doubt if we get back till the twenty-eighth. I am a bit exhausted but really all right." "We" this time included his daughter Anna.

When President Roosevelt addressed Congress on the first of March to report to them on the results of Yalta, he did something he had never done before. He spoke sitting down to avoid the strain of standing in his leg braces.

To gather all of the strength that he knew he would need for the opening of the San Francisco Conference, FDR took an "off the record" vacation at Warm Springs, arriving there on the thirtieth of March. Fala was with him. Those in Warm Springs who had not seen him in many weeks gasped a little to notice how much the

President had failed and how tired he looked. But the piney air, the Georgia sun, and swimming in the warm pool began to restore him almost at once.

April first was Easter Sunday, and he took deep pleasure in attending worship in the Foundation's Chapel that morning. During the following week he answered mail, received visitors, talked of his plans for the San Francisco Conference, plans for a barbecue at Warm Springs. On the afternoon of Wednesday the eleventh he wrote the first draft of a speech he was to give at a Jefferson Day dinner on Friday.

During the late morning of April 12 he sat before his fireplace, papers of state spread before him on a card table, reading and working. At the other end of the room the painter, Madame Elizabeth Shoumatoff, stood working before a large canvas sketching in the beginnings of a portrait of the President. She had draped a navy blue cape around his shoulders. Now and again she tried to engage him in conversation to catch the different expressions of his face.

There were other people in the room, but they did not distract the President or the painter. His cousin who had given him Fala, Miss Margaret Suckley, was sitting on the couch crocheting quietly. Miss Laura Delano, another cousin, was arranging flowers in vases around the room. A maid was setting the table for luncheon.

Suddenly the President pressed his hand to his forehead; then he rubbed the back of his neck.

"I have a terrific headache," he said.

Miss Suckley heard him and looked up.

His left arm seemed to go limp, his head dropped forward, and he slumped over the arm of his chair—unconscious.

His two cousins rushed to support him.

"Ask the Secret Service man to call a doctor immediately," said Miss Suckley to the artist. Madame Shoumatoff raced out of the door.

But Miss Suckley herself snatched the phone from its cradle and told the operator to call a doctor, and in a few minutes Dr. Howard Bruenn came rushing up from the treatment pool.

The President's valet and others carried him to his bed. The doctor hurriedly cut away his clothing, giving what treatment he could, and to the anxious frightened faces about him he said, "It was a cerebral hemorrhage."

President Roosevelt never regained consciousness. An hour and twenty minutes after his attack he was dead.

The suddenness of it shocked everyone into helplessness for a few moments, until they began to realize how much was involved. Then phone calls were made to the White House, to the State Department, to the newspapers.

Before boarding a plane for Warm Springs, Eleanor Roosevelt sent a telegram to each of her children:

"Darlings: Pa slept away this afternoon. He did his job

to the end as he would want you to do. Bless you. All our love. Mother."

Franklin Delano Roosevelt's funeral and burial were in accordance with exact wishes that he had expressed to his family many years before. The services, first at the White House, and then at Hyde Park, were plain and simple. He lies in the center of a green square of lawn on his own estate, behind the privacy of hemlock hedge, in the Hudson River Valley.

Among the papers on his desk at the Little White House was the speech he had written for the Jefferson Day dinner. Its closing words were:

"To all Americans who dedicate themselves with us to the making of an abiding peace, I say: The only limit to our realization of tomorrow will be our doubts of today. Let us move forward with strong and active faith."

Chapter Fourteen

Two Great Dreams Coming True

THREE DAYS AFTER the President's death, special trains began to travel from various ports and cities of the United States to San Francisco. They were carrying nearly five thousand persons, delegates and staffs, of forty-six nations. In San Francisco they would hold the history making sessions to which the Big Three had agreed.

The Big Three by now had become the Big Five: the United States, represented by Secretary of State Edward R. Stettinius, Jr.; the United Kingdom represented by Foreign Secretary Sir Anthony Eden; the Soviet Union represented by Foreign Commissar Vyacheslav M. Molotov; China represented by Foreign Minister Dr. T. V. Soong; and France represented by Minister of Foreign Affairs Georges Bidault. Secretary Stettinius,

226

who had been Undersecretary of State until ill health
forced Cordell Hull to retire at the end of 1944, became
President of the Conference.

On opening day, April 25, 1945, President Harry S.
Truman addressed the delegates by telephone from the
White House. Cordell Hull sent a message saying that
this Conference would be the "acid test" to show whether
or not mankind had learned its lesson.

The Sessions lasted for two months. There were many
disagreements and points of difference to be ironed out
before a Charter of the United Nations, based on the
preliminary work done at Dumbarton Oaks, could be
drafted. But when at last the Charter was completed, the
nations assembled approved it unanimously.

The Charter provided for a General Assembly which
all member nations would attend, an International Court
of Justice, and a Security Council. Eleven nations would
have membership on the Security Council; the Big Five
would have permanent membership; the other six seats
would revolve among the rest of the countries. The
Council would be the top executive group, making the
most important plans and decisions.

Under these three principal divisions—the Court, the
Assembly, and the Security Council—there were to be
special Commissions (statistics, human rights, employment, control of narcotics, communications) and Specialized Agencies (World Health Organization, International Refugee Organization, International Trade Organ-

ization, United Nations Economic and Social Council or UNESCO, International Labor Organization). Most important of all, the Charter provided that the United Nations could grow and change to meet changing needs and times.

On May 7, 1945, while the San Francisco Conference was still going on, Germany surrendered and brought the war in Europe to a close. By early autumn the war in the Pacific was over. Preliminary tasks of writing peace treaties and determining boundaries were performed by a Council of Foreign Ministers, composed of the Big Five.

The event that did greatest honor to the memory of Franklin Delano Roosevelt occurred in January, 1946, the opening of the first sessions of the United Nations. The General Assembly convened on the tenth and the Security Council on the seventeenth, in London. To honor his memory still further, Mrs. Eleanor Roosevelt became a member of the United States delegation to the United Nations and chairman of the Commission on Human Rights. She continued her devoted work with the United Nations until 1952. In March, 1961, Mrs. Roosevelt was named a representative of the United States to the 15th session of the General Assembly of the United Nations.

The first and most pressing task of the new world organization was emergency relief to the starving and homeless in war-devastated countries and the rebuilding of roads, bridges, houses, and communications.

During its existence, the United Nations has been able

to assume more and more responsibility and to win more and more trust and respect from the world. It has mediated a long list of international disputes any one of which could have drawn other nations into warfare: the Palestine question, the disagreement between India and Pakistan over Kashmir, the Berlin blockade, the invasion of South Korea by North Korea, the Congo crisis.

But the mediation of conflicts has been only one of its contributions. Realizing that conflict is the end result, the symptom of conditions, and not the cause itself, the special agencies of the U. N. are working constantly to cure the causes of war: poverty, oppression, sickness, misunderstandings among peoples. The U. N. has set up special commissions on the different continents to study economic conditions and ways to raise standards of living. It now has a ten-nation Committee on Disarmament, an International Conference on the Peaceful Uses of Atomic Energy, and a Committee on Peaceful Uses of Outer Space.

The special agency that would have been closest to FDR's heart is UNICEF, the United Nations International Children's Fund. UNICEF began as a temporary agency after the war and was soon made permanent. It was fifteen years old in December, 1961. UNICEF provides milk and vitamins and disease-preventing vaccines to children all over the world. It studies their health problems and sends doctors and nurses into areas where they are needed. FDR had always loved children. He could never bear to know that they were suffering or neglected in any way, and being stricken with a children's disease made him more deeply concerned than ever for their health.

It was his own illness that gave rise to his second dream: the conquest of that most painful and crippling of blights: polio. Georgia Warm Springs Foundation and The National Foundation have gone on to great achievements because of the inspiration that he gave them.

The quadrangle of fireproof buildings at Warm Springs is completed. Roosevelt Hall was opened in 1953 and the Children's Pavilion in 1955. On the façade of Roosevelt Hall there are two pictures in bas relief. To the left of the entrance are the figures of the deaf-blind Helen Keller and her teacher, Anne Sullivan Macy, and under them the legend: "While they were saying among themselves it cannot be done, it was done." To the right of the entrance is President Roosevelt in his chair talking to a child on crutches, and the legend: "There is nothing to fear but fear itself."

Warm Springs has expanded its services with its facilities. It treats those suffering from a wide variety of handicaps: birth defects, arthritis, injuries suffered in accidents. And it is a training place for student therapists who come to Warm Springs from all over the world so that they can carry their new skills back to their own countries. There is no place in the world quite like Georgia Warm Springs Foundation.

As an added memorial, the Little White House has been made a public shrine that travelers may visit. The house is just as it was when FDR lived in it. Madame Shoumatoff's unfinished portrait still stands on its easel in the living room. On the same grounds the summer home of Miss Georgia Wilkins has been made into a museum. In it are displayed Madame Shoumatoff's finished second portrait of the President, painted after his death. There are long cases filled with his personal possessions, gifts from everyone imaginable, and hundreds of canes that were presented to him from time to time, sometimes beautifully hand carved. The Museum and the Little White House are owned and operated by the State of Georgia.

The National Foundation in New York, with its 3,100 chapters throughout the country, is responsible almost entirely for the progress that has been made against polio in the last twenty years. It has provided the funds for research, training, equipment, medical care, and free vaccine. Now that polio is on the wane, it has extended its efforts into the fields of birth defects and arthritis.

Basil O'Connor, who has been President of The National Foundation since its founding, has been called "the architect of the fight against polio." His vision has been as worldwide and as long-ranged as FDR's. Three years after President Roosevelt's death, he organized the First International Poliomyelitis Conference in New York City. Scientists attended from forty-three countries to pool all of their knowledge and experience on the disease. These world conferences on polio have been held every three years ever since—in Copenhagen, Rome, Geneva, and again in Copenhagen in 1960.

Six months after the first world conference on polio, scientists working with National Foundation aid at the Children's Hospital at Back Bay, Boston, published a discovery that the polio virus could be made to grow in non-nervous tissue. This was such an important break-through that the three physicians, Dr. John Enders, Dr. Thomas Weller, and Dr. Frederick Robbins, eventually received the Nobel prize in medicine for their discovery. By 1952 Dr. William McD. Hammon of the University of Pittsburgh developed gamma globulin to provide some temporary protection against paralytic polio. In another year Dr. Jonas E. Salk at the same university announced that he hoped that a preliminary killed-virus vaccine that he had developed would give a high degree of immunity. In 1954 came the famous field trials of the Salk vaccine, again financed by The National Foundation, in which nearly two million school children participated. When Dr. Salk's vaccine was declared to be from 60 to 90 per cent effective, The National Foundation provided it free to millions of children in the first and second grades.

Dr. Salk did not stop there. He went on working to improve the effectiveness of his vaccine. Other research scientists did not stop either. Many years earlier they had learned that there are three types of polio virus and that all three must be used to make a vaccine. At long last, in 1955 the tiny polio virus was identified with the help of the electron microscope. Scientists could at last *look* at the organism that caused polio.

The newest work is being done on a live-virus vaccine, that may be taken orally in a pill or syrup. Most outstanding in this field is Dr. Albert Sabin of the University of Cincinnati College of Medicine. He has developed the Sabin vaccine with National Foundation grants. Field trials with the Sabin vaccine have already been made; the American Medical Association has approved it; and the Surgeon General of the United States who is head of the Public Health Service has approved it for licensing.

The battle against polio is well on its way to victory, but it cannot be won until everyone is inoculated, and nearly half the population of the United States has not yet had any vaccine. While the greatest number of polio's victims are children and it seldom attacks anyone over forty-five years of age, it could attack anybody.

Before the Salk vaccine was used an average of nearly forty thousand persons a year in the United States were being stricken with polio. In 1960 there were only around three thousand cases. Some day there will be none—anywhere in the world.

Thus, FDR's two greatest dreams are coming true: a world organization to create world peace and the conquest of polio.

"Let us move forward with strong and active faith."

Selected Bibliography

ARNE, SIGRID. *United Nations Primer.* New York: Rinehart & Company, Inc., 1948.

ASBELL, BERNARD. *When F.D.R. Died.* New York: Holt, Rinehart and Winston, Inc., 1961.

ASHBURN, FRANK D. *Peabody of Groton.* New York: Coward McCann, Inc., 1944.

BECKEL, GRAHAM. *Workshops for the World, The Specialized Agencies of the United Nations.* New York: Abelard-Schuman, 1954.

BURNS, JAMES MACGREGOR. *Roosevelt: The Lion and the Fox.* New York: Harcourt, Brace and Company, 1956.

COHN, VICTOR. *Four Billion Dimes.* Minneapolis: Minneapolis Star and Tribune, n.d.

COX, JAMES M. *Journey Through My Years.* New York: Simon and Schuster, 1946.

DANIELS, JOSEPHUS. *The Wilson Era, Years of Peace 1910–1917.* Chapel Hill: The University of North Carolina Press, 1944.

DILLON, MARY EARHART. *Wendell Willkie.* Philadelphia: J. B. Lippincott Company, 1952.

Dows, Olin. *Franklin Roosevelt at Hyde Park*. New York: American Artists Group, Inc., 1949.

Draper, George, M. D. *Infantile Paralysis*. New York: D. Appleton–Century Company, Incorporated, 1935.

Freidel, Frank. *Franklin D. Roosevelt*. Volume I, *The Apprenticeship*; Volume II, *The Ordeal*; Volume III, *The Triumph*. Boston: Little, Brown and Company, 1952, 1954, and 1956.

Halsey, Fleet Admiral William F., and Lieutenant Commander J. Bryan, III. *Admiral Halsey's Story*. New York: Whittlesey House, 1947.

Handlin, Oscar. *Al Smith and His America*. Boston: Little, Brown and Company, 1958.

Hassett, William D. *Off the Record with FDR 1942–1945*. New Brunswick: Rutgers University Press, 1958.

Heckscher, August (Editor). *The Politics of Woodrow Wilson*. New York: Harper & Brothers, 1956.

Hinton, Harold B. *Cordell Hull*. Garden City: Doubleday, Doran & Company, Inc., 1942.

Kilpatrick, Carroll. *Roosevelt and Daniels, A Friendship in Politics*. Chapel Hill: The University of North Carolina Press, 1952.

Lewis, William Draper. *The Life of Theodore Roosevelt*. Philadelphia: The John C. Winston Company, 1919.

Lindley, Ernest K. *Franklin D. Roosevelt, A Career in Progressive Democracy*. Indianapolis: The Bobbs-Merrill Company, 1931.

Link, Arthur S. *Wilson, The Road to the White House*. Princeton: Princeton University Press, 1947.

———. *Wilson, The New Freedom*. Princeton: Princeton University Press, 1956.

McIntire, Vice-Admiral Ross T. *White House Physician*. New York: G. P. Putnam's Sons, 1946.

Morison, Samuel Eliot. *Three Centuries of Harvard 1636–1936*. Cambridge: Harvard University Press, 1936.

PERKINS, FRANCES. *The Roosevelt I Knew.* New York: The Viking Press, 1946.

ROOSEVELT, ELEANOR, and HELEN FERRIS. *Partners, The United Nations and Youth.* Garden City: Doubleday & Co., Inc., 1950.

————. *This I Remember.* New York: Harper & Brothers, 1949.

————. *This Is My Story.* New York: Harper & Brothers, 1937.

ROOSEVELT, ELLIOTT. *As He Saw It.* New York: Duell, Sloan and Pearce, 1946.

ROOSEVELT, FRANKLIN DELANO. *F.D.R. His Personal Letters,* Three Volumes in Four, Edited by Elliott Roosevelt. New York: Duell, Sloan and Pearce, 1950.

————. *Nothing to Fear, The Selected Addresses* (1932–1945) *of Franklin Delano Roosevelt,* Edited by B. D. Zevin. Boston: Houghton Mifflin Company, 1946.

ROOSEVELT, MRS. JAMES. *My Boy Franklin.* New York: Ray Long & Richard R. Smith, Inc., 1933.

ROOSEVELT, JAMES, and SIDNEY SHALETT. *Affectionately, F.D.R.* New York: Harcourt, Brace & Company, 1959.

ROSENMAN, SAMUEL I. *Working with Roosevelt.* New York: Harper & Brothers, 1952.

SCHLESINGER, ARTHUR M., JR. *The Age of Roosevelt.* Volume I, *The Crisis of the Old Order 1919–1933;* Volume II, *The Coming of the New Deal;* Volume III, *The Politics of Upheaval.* Boston: Houghton Mifflin Company, 1957, 1959, and 1960.

SHERWOOD, ROBERT E. *Roosevelt and Hopkins.* New York: Harper & Brothers, 1948.

SILLS, DAVID L. *The Volunteers.* Glencoe: Free Press, 1957.

STEEHOLM, CLARA and HARDY. *The House at Hyde Park.* New York: The Viking Press, 1950.

STEINBERG, ALFRED. *Mrs. R: The Life of Eleanor Roosevelt.* New York: G. P. Putnam's Sons, 1958.

STEVENS, RUTH. *Hi-Ya Neighbor.* New York: Tupper and Love, Inc., 1947.

STILES, LELA. *The Man Behind Roosevelt.* Cleveland: The World Publishing Company, 1954.

SUCKLEY, MARGARET. *The True Story of Fala.* New York: Charles Scribner's Sons, 1942.

TULLY, GRACE. *F.D.R. My Boss.* New York: Charles Scribner's Sons, 1949.

VANDENBOSCH, AMRY, and WILLARD N. HOGAN. *The United Nations.* New York: McGraw-Hill Book Company, Inc., 1952.

VAN SINDEREN, ADRIAN. *Four Years, A Chronicle of the War by Months.* New York: Coward-McCann, Inc., 1944.

WAGNER, CHARLES A. *Harvard: Four Centuries and Freedoms.* New York: E. P. Dutton & Company, Inc., 1950.

WALKER, TURNLEY. *Roosevelt and the Warm Springs Story.* New York: A. A. Wyn, Inc., 1953.

WALWORTH, ARTHUR. *Woodrow Wilson.* Volume I, *American Prophet;* Volume II, *World Prophet.* New York, Longmans, Green and Co., 1958.

WILLIAMS, GREER. *Virus Hunters.* New York: Alfred A. Knopf, 1959.

Index

Acheson, Dean, 175
Agricultural Adjustment Act
    (AAA), 178, 192, 193
Atlantic Charter, 213–214,
    217

Balkan Wars, 82, 85
Baruch, Bernard, 175
Bennet, E. H., Dr., 84, 113–
    114
Berle, Adolf A., Jr., 175
Bethune, Mary McLeod, 189
Bidault, Georges, 226
"Big Three, The," 216, 222,
    226
Botts, Fred, 143
Brandeis, Louis, Justice, 192
Brodie, Maurice, Dr., 185

Brown, Lathrop, 25, 30, 36,
    38, 53, 56, 78, 80, 94
Bull Moosers, 77
Bulloch, Minnie, 138

Campobello Island, 4, 25, 27,
    48, 54, 74, 76, 82, 84, 90,
    111
Cantor, Eddie, 201–202
Carter, Ledyard & Milburn,
    60
Casablanca, 218
Chief, 98, 143
Churchill, Winston, 206,
    211–213, 216, 217, 218,
    220, 221, 222
Civil Works Administration
    (CWA), 177–178, 193

Civilian Conservation Corps (CCC), 176–177
Clark, Champ, 73–75
Columbia University, 54, 59, 60
conservation, 67–68, 176–177
Coolidge, Calvin, 102, 109, 132
Cowles, William Sheffield, Mrs. (Aunt Bye, Cousin Bammie), 25, 53
Cox, James M., 105–106, 107, 109
Cross, Guernsey, 158
Curtis, Egbert T., 148

Dall, Curtis, 148, 159
Daniels, Josephus, 72, 78–79, 83, 86, 94, 119
Debby, 10
De Gaulle, Charles, General, 218, 220
Delano, Warren (uncle), 2
Democratic National Conventions, 1912, 71–75; 1920, 103–106; 1924, 130–135; 1928, 151; 1932, 162–167; 1940, 207–208; 1944, 220
depression, 159, 160–161, 172–200
Dewey, Thomas E., 206–207
Disarmament Conference, 188
Draper, George, Dr., 117, 118

Duffy, 59, 62

Early, Stephen T., 108
Eden, Anthony, Sir, 226
Eisenhower, Dwight, General, 218
Eliot, Charles W., 41
Emergency Banking Act, 176
Emmett, Marvin and Roosevelt, 110
Enders, John, Dr., 232

Fala, 209–210, 222
Farley, James A., 162, 167, 169, 175, 192, 208
Federal Bank Deposit Insurance Corp., 181
Federal Emergency Relief Act (FERA), 177
Fidelity and Deposit Company of Maryland, 110, 128
Fly (Alpha Delta Phi), 40, 48, 49
Ford, Edsel, 152
"Fourteen Points," 95
Frankfurter, Felix, 158

Georgia Warm Springs Foundation (*see also* Warm Springs), 146–149, 173, 184, 210, 230–234
Groton School, 14, 15–37, 99, 126, 153

Grotonian, 32, 34, 39

Half Moon I, 5, 25, 34
Half Moon II, 48, 60, 99
Hall, Anna (Eleanor Roosevelt's mother), 13, 57
Halsey, William F., Jr., 82
Hammon, William McD., Dr., 232
Harding, Warren G., 103
Hart, William, 138, 140, 145
Harvard Crimson, The, 39, 40, 41, 42, 43–44, 50
Harvard Republican Club, 40
Harvard Union, 44–45, 48, 50
Harvard University, 15, 36, 38–54
Hasty Pudding, 40, 48, 49
Hoover, Herbert, 86, 96, 153, 156, 162, 168, 197
Hopkins, Harry, 160, 177, 212, 215
Howe, Louis McHenry, 77–78, 81, 108, 113–114, 117–118, 124, 125, 143, 148, 156, 160, 162, 165, 169, 182, 192
Hubbard, LeRoy W., Dr., 147, 152
Hudson River (and Valley), 1, 13, 67, 127, 207, 225
Hughes, Charles E., Chief Justice, 198

Hull, Cordell, 158, 175, 188, 197, 206, 208, 214, 215, 227
Hyde Park (*see also* Springwood), 3, 9, 51, 56, 62, 76, 91, 109, 128, 157, 168, 194, 209, 225

Ickes, Harold, 175, 189
infantile paralysis, *see* poliomyelitis

Joseph, Louis, 136, 138, 139, 143

Keen, W. W., Dr., 114
King, Ernest, Admiral, 218
Knox, Frank, 206, 215
Kolmer, John, Dr., 185
Ku Klux Klan, 131, 132, 137

Landon, Alfred M., 193–194
Larooco, 145
Lawrence, James, Mr. & Mrs., 16, 19
League of Nations, 95, 101–102, 105, 131, 132
Le Hand, Marguerite ("Missy"), 110, 124, 125, 137, 140, 152, 154, 156, 162, 182, 214
Lehman, Herbert H., 154, 155
Lend-Lease, 211, 214
Little White House, 172, 190, 223–225, 231

Lovett, Robert W., Dr., 115–117, 124
Loyless, Tom, 137, 140, 144, 145

McAdoo, William Gibbs, 105, 134, 164
MacArthur, Douglas, General, 219
McDonald, William, Dr., 123–124, 143–144, 149
McIntire, Ross T., Vice-Admiral, 183, 214, 221
McIntyre, Marvin, 108, 167
McKinley, William, 24, 40, 41, 45
Mahoney, Helena T., 147, 152
March of Dimes, 202, 210
Marksman (dog), 10
Marshall, George C., General, 212, 215, 218
Marvin, Hooker & Roosevelt, 68
Meriwether Inn, 137, 138, 142, 146
Moley, Raymond, 175, 198
Molotov, Vyacheslav M., 226
Morgenthau, Henry, Jr., and Elinor, 127, 156, 157, 175, 206

National Foundation, The, 201–202, 217, 230–234

National Recovery Administration (NRA), 181–182, 185, 190–192, 193, 199
National Youth Administration (NYA), 189, 193
Neutrality Act, 203
Newbold, Mary, 13
New Deal, 166, 171 ff
Nimitz, Chester, Admiral, 219
Norris, George, 179–180

O'Connor, Basil, 129–130, 141, 144, 146, 148, 173, 175, 201, 231–232

Paris Peace Conference, 100
Peabody, Endicott, Rev., 17, 21, 37, 56, 168, 195
Peabody, George Foster, 136, 137, 141, 144, 148
Pearl Harbor, 28, 215
Perkins, Frances, 157, 159, 175, 197
poliomyelitis, 89–91, 121–122, 185–186, 201, 210–211, 230, 231–233
Porcellian, 39, 43, 48
Presbyterian Hospital, 117, 118–119
Presidential Inaugurations, 78, 79, 173–175, 195, 221–222
Prohibition, 132, 159, 161

Public Works Administration (PWA), 189, 193

Raskob, John J., 155
Red Cross, 93, 100, 125, 217
Reid, Jean, 50, 58
Reid, Whitelaw, 50
Republican National Conventions, 1900, 40; 1912, 73, 77; 1920, 103; 1924, 132; 1932, 162; 1940, 206–207
Robbins, Frederick, Dr., 232
Roberts, Owen J., Justice, 191
Rogers, Edmund, 6, 14, 15, 18, 20
Roosevelt, Anna Eleanor (daughter) (*see also* Dall, Curtis), 59–60, 62, 98–99, 109, 143, 148, 162, 165, 218
Roosevelt, Anna Eleanor (wife), 6, 7, 13, 14, 33–34, 46–48, 51–54, 55–59, 61, 74, 93, 99–102, 108, 119, 125, 143, 153–154, 159, 163, 171, 180–181, 182, 194, 215, 217, 224–225, 228
Roosevelt, Elliott (Mrs. Roosevelt's brother), 57
Roosevelt, Elliott (Mrs. Roosevelt's father,

Roosevelt, Elliott (*cont.*)
FDR's godfather), 6, 13, 57–58, 159
Roosevelt, Elliott (son), 64, 86, 109, 126, 151, 162, 211, 212, 218
Roosevelt, Franklin Delano:
appearance, 3–4, 27, 32, 36, 39, 123, 129, 133, 221, 223
Asst. Secy. of Navy, 78–102
birds, love of, 10, 34
birth, 1, 3
boats and ships, love of, 4, 5, 79, 82
at Casablanca, 218
meetings with Churchill, 211–213, 217, 218, 221, 222
at Columbia University, 54, 59, 60
death, 223–225
engagement, 51
creates Georgia Warm Springs Foundation, 146–149
Governor of New York, 152–162
Groton, 14, 15–37
Harvard University, 38–54
creates National Foundation, 201–202
New York Senator, 63–68
has polio, 113 ff

Roosevelt, Franklin (*cont.*)
political comeback, 131–135
President, 168 ff
stamp collecting, 12, 34, 186
at Teheran, 219
runs for U. S. Senate, 83–84, 85
runs for Vice Presidency, 105–106
wedding, 55–59
at Yalta, 222
Roosevelt, Franklin Delano, Jr. (first son of this name), 62
Roosevelt, Franklin Delano, Jr. (second son of this name), 84, 86, 109, 159, 162, 165, 211, 212, 218
Roosevelt, Hall (Mrs. Roosevelt's brother), 57
Roosevelt, James (father), 1, 2, 5, 15, 24, 26, 35–36, 40, 42
Roosevelt, James (son), 61, 86, 99, 109, 132, 159, 162, 165, 167, 169–170, 211, 215, 218, 221
Roosevelt, James Roosevelt (half brother), 2
Roosevelt, John Aspinwall (son), 89, 109, 153, 159, 162, 165, 211, 218

Roosevelt, Sara Delano (mother), 1, 2, 5, 13, 23, 26, 31, 42, 52–54, 55, 61, 77, 109, 116, 214
Roosevelt, Taddy (nephew), 16, 20, 25
Roosevelt, Theodore (cousin), 12, 15, 24, 25–26, 29, 31, 40, 43–44, 51, 55–56, 73, 77, 78, 80, 101
Roosevelt, Theodore, Jr., 109
Roosevelt and O'Connor, 129
Rosenman, Samuel I., 156, 157, 162, 164, 175, 194
Rural Electrification Administration (REA), 189, 190

Sabin, Albert, Dr., 233
St. James' Church, 3, 9, 62
St. Lawrence Seaway, 158
Salk, Jonas E., Dr., 217, 232–233
San Francisco Conference, 222, 226–230
Shoumatoff, Elizabeth, 223–224, 231
Smith, Alfred E., 103–105, 127–128, 150, 151, 154, 161, 163
Social Security Act, 190, 196
Soong, T. V., Dr., 226
Spanish-American War, 28–31

Springwood, 3, 4, 5
Stalin, Joseph, 216, 219, 220, 222
Stark, Harold R., 82
Stettinius, Edward R., Jr., 226–227
Stimson, Henry L., 206, 215
Straus, Jesse, 160
Suckley, Margaret, 209, 223–224
Supreme Court, U. S., 190–192, 195–198

Taft, William Howard, 73, 78
Tammany Hall, 60, 66–67, 74–75, 83, 107, 127–128
Teheran, 219
Temporary Emergency Relief Administration (TERA), 160
Tennessee Valley Authority (TVA), 178–181, 192, 193
Thompson, Malvina, 125, 162, 182
Truman, Harry S., 227
Tugwell, Rexford G., 175
Tully, Grace, 156, 162, 182, 183, 215

Underwood, Oscar, 73–75
United Nations, 186–187, 200, 217, 220–221, 222, 226–230

Van Devanter, Willis, Justice, 198
Vireo, 110, 112

Wagner Labor Relations Act, 190, 198
Wallace, Henry, 175
Warm Springs (*see also* Georgia Warm Springs Foundation), 136–149, 151–155, 156, 171, 172, 221, 223–225, 230–231
Weller, Thomas, Dr., 232
Welles, Sumner, 212–213
Weona II, 130
Wilkins, Georgia, 138, 210
Williams, Aubrey, 189
Willkie, Wendell, 180, 192, 206
Wilson, Woodrow, 66, 69–75, 78, 79, 83, 87–88, 91, 92, 95, 100, 101–103, 107–108
Woodrow Wilson Foundation, The, 124, 144
Works Progress Administration (WPA), 189, 193
World Court, 188
World War I, 85–100
World War II, 203 ff

Yalta, 222

About the Author

Catherine Owens Peare has always been interested in writing. She was the editor of her high school paper and in college she wrote plays and poetry. After graduation Miss Peare went to work on Wall Street but she continued to write on evenings and week ends. Her books for young people have been so well received she now devotes all her time to writing.

Miss Peare lives in Brooklyn, New York, and travels a great deal throughout Europe, Central America, and the United States, combining pleasure with research for future books.